MW00628454

studies in jazz

Institute of Jazz Studies
Rutgers—The State University of New Jersey
General Editors: Dan Morgenstern and Edward Berger

1. BENNY CARTER: A Life in American Music, *by Morroe Berger, Edward Berger, and James Patrick, 1982*
2. ART TATUM: A Guide to His Recorded Music, *by Arnold Laubich and Ray Spencer, 1982*
3. ERROLL GARNER: The Most Happy Piano, *by James M. Doran,* 1995
4. JAMES P. JOHNSON: A Case of Mistaken Identity, *by Scott E. Brown;* Discography 1917–1950, *by Robert Hilbert,* 1986
5. PEE WEE ERWIN: This Horn for Hire, *as told to Warren W. Vaché, Sr.,* 1987
6. BENNY GOODMAN: Listen to His Legacy, *by D. Russell Connor,* 1988
7. ELLINGTONIA: The Recorded Music of Duke Ellington and His Sidemen, *by W. E. Timner,* 1988; 4th ed., 1996
8. THE GLENN MILLER ARMY AIR FORCE BAND: Sustineo Alas/ I Sustain the Wings, *by Edward F. Polic;* Foreword *by George T. Simon,* 1989
9. SWING LEGACY, *by Chip Deffaa,* 1989
10. REMINISCING IN TEMPO: The Life and Times of a Jazz Hustler, *by Teddy Reig, with Edward Berger,* 1990
11. IN THE MAINSTREAM: 18 Portraits in Jazz, *by Chip Deffaa,* 1992
12. BUDDY DeFRANCO: A Biographical Portrait and Discography, *by John Kuehn and Arne Astrup,* 1993
13. PEE WEE SPEAKS: A Discography of Pee Wee Russell, *by Robert Hilbert, with David Niven,* 1992
14. SYLVESTER AHOLA: The Gloucester Gabriel, *by Dick Hill,* 1993
15. THE POLICE CARD DISCORD, *by Maxwell T. Cohen,* 1993
16. TRADITIONALISTS AND REVIVALISTS IN JAZZ, *by Chip Deffaa,* 1993
17. BASSICALLY SPEAKING: An Oral History of George Duvivier, *by Edward Berger;* Musical Analysis *by David Chevan,* 1993
18. TRAM: The Frank Trumbauer Story, *by Philip R. Evans and Larry F. Kiner, with William Trumbauer,* 1994
19. TOMMY DORSEY: On the Side, *by Robert L. Stockdale,* 1995
20. JOHN COLTRANE: A Discography and Musical Biography, *by Yasuhiro Fujioka, with Lewis Porter and Yoh-ichi Hamada,* 1995

21. RED HEAD: A Chronological Survey of "Red" Nichols and His Five Pennies, *by Stephen M. Stroff,* 1995
22. THE RED NICHOLS STORY: After Intermission 1942–1965, *by Stanley Hester, Stephen Hester, Philip Evans, and Linda Evans,* 1996
23. BENNY GOODMAN: Wrappin' It Up, *by D. Russell Connor,* 1996
24. CHARLIE PARKER AND THEMATIC IMPROVISATION, *by Henry Martin,* 1996

Charlie Parker and Thematic Improvisation

Henry Martin

The Scarecrow Press, Inc.
Lanham, Maryland, and London
2001

SCARECROW PRESS, INC.

Published in the United States of America
by Scarecrow Press, Inc.
4720 Boston Way, Lanham, Maryland 20706
www.scarecrowpress.com

4 Pleydell Gardens, Folkestone
Kent CT20 2DN, England

British Library Cataloguing in Publication Information Available

The hardback edition of this book was previously cataloged by the Library of
Congress as follows:

Martin, Henry, 1950-
Charlie Parker and thematic improvisation / by Henry Martin.
p.   cm. – (Studies in jazz; no. 24)
Includes bibliographical references, discography, and index.
1. Parker, Charlie, 1920-1955—Criticism and interpretation. 2. Improvisation
(Music). 3. Jazz—Analysis, appreciation. I. Title. II. Series.
ML 419.P4M37   1996   788.7'3165'092—dc20   95-49636

ISBN: 0-8108-4155-X (paper)

Manufactured in the United States of America.

For my wonderful parents, Mary Martin and Henry Martin, Sr.

Contents

Editor's Foreword   ix
Foreword   xi
Acknowledgments   xiii

Chapter 1: Introduction   1
Formula and Thematic Improvisation   1
Transcriptions   5

Chapter 2: Improvisation and Linear Theory   9
Strophic Form and Harmonic Prolongation   9
Voice-leading Models   13
Larger-scale Structure and Thematic Patterns   20
Types of Thematic Patterns   32
Thematic Pattern, Motive and Formula in Improvisation   34

Chapter 3: Rhythm Changes   41
Rhythm Changes as a Formal Model   41
Red Cross   42
   Red Cross—Original Melody   42
   Red Cross—Take 1   44
   Red Cross—Take 2   47
Shaw 'Nuff   48
   Shaw 'Nuff—Original Melody   48
   Shaw 'Nuff—Improvisation   51
   Shaw 'Nuff—Other Improvisational Features   54
Thriving on a Riff   57
   Thriving on a Riff—Original Melody   58
   Thriving on a Riff—Take 1   59
   Thriving on a Riff—Take 3   61
Crazeology   64
Wee   66
Lester Leaps In   68

Chapter 4: Popular Song   71
Embraceable You   71
   Embraceable You—Original Melody   71

Embraceable You—Take 1   72
Embraceable You—Take 2   78
Just Friends   82
Just Friends—Original Melody   83
Just Friends—Studio Improvisation   84
Just Friends—Café Society ("Pop")   89
Cherokee and Koko   93
Star Eyes   95

Chapter 5: The Blues   **99**
Cool Blues   100
Perhaps   102
Au Privave   105
Blues for Alice   105
Bongo Bop   106
Now's the Time   107
Cheryl   107
Parker's Mood   107

Chapter 6: Master Soloist   **111**
General Style Considerations   111
Quotation   114
Other Issues in Thematic Reference   114
Formula and Its Ramifications   115
Thematic Reference   115
Parallels in Oral-Epic Poetry   121
Literacy and its Role in the Jazz Tradition   122
Large-Scale Impact on Contemporary Music   125
Parker's Balance of Formula and Traditional Western Values   128

Works Cited   **131**
Bibliography   131
Discography   133

Notes   135
Index   151
About the Author   155

Editor's Foreword

Henry Martin's principal task in this book consists of showing that the standard view of Charlie Parker as connecting melodic formulas together in creative ways to fashion his solos does not do justice to the greatness of his work. Indeed, Martin shows that while the solos do contain much melodic formula, Parker's ear was still engaged by the melody of the original song. Martin goes on to explore the broader implications of this theory by touching on the nature of improvisation itself, examining such terms as "paraphrase" and "formula," and confronting the issue of Parker's quotation from other material.

It has been a great pleasure for me to work on this project with Henry—a musician with unusually broad interests, whose background and capabilities equip him superbly to undertake the study of Parker's music. As a concert music composer who has taught jazz at Princeton, and now directs music theory and composition at the New School-Mannes Jazz Program, he is perhaps the ideal musician to bring to jazz the techniques derived from the study of the Western concert tradition.

This volume expands the purview of the *Studies in Jazz* series as it is the first to focus primarily on analysis. The previous volumes have already covered a wide range of artists from the viewpoints of biography, discography, and oral history. Future volumes are being developed that study various modern jazz artists and involve more technical musical analysis.

Lewis Porter
Associate Professor of Music
Rutgers University

Foreword

It might seem that during the past twenty years most of the obstacles to a full examination of Charlie Parker's art were overcome. Nearly all of his known recordings have become available on commercial discs. In particular, the five largest, distinct blocks of material have been issued in complete, systematically organized compact disc editions—the Dial, Savoy, Verve, Deae Benedetti, and the 1948–1949 Royal Roost broadcasts—some 782 items in all. In addition, many of the remaining live and private recordings have been presented in chronological order in the JUTB 18-compact disc Bird Box collection. The Parker recordings have been codified in carefully-prepared discographies and hundreds of notated transcriptions of his solos have been published. Numerous photos and documents appeared for the first time in Chan Parker's and Francis Paudras's luxurious picture book *To Bird with Love* (1982). Parker has been extensively covered in the premier musical encyclopedias of our time and is the subject of both a fine video, "Celebrating Bird" (1988), based on Gary Giddins's 1987 biography, and a controversial Hollywood feature film, Clint Eastwood's "Bird" (1988). As I write these words, Christie's in London is auctioning items pictured in the Parker-Paudras book with sales expected to exceed £ 120,000.

The ironic curiosity remains that Parker's music itself—the ultimate source of all this obeisance—has been so little studied. In hindsight, it seems almost touching how thrilling it was to read the first modest attempts at a *musical* assessment of Bird or to purchase the first published transcriptions of his solos. I refer, in particular, to André Hodeir's sensitive chapter in *Jazz: Its Evolution and Essence* (first published in English in 1956) and Don Heckman's essay "Bird in Flight," included as part of a 1965 Parker memorial issue of *Down Beat*. Many years passed before two important, first-rate, book-length studies appeared: Thomas Owens's 1974 U.C.L.A. two-volume doctoral dissertation, "Charlie Parker: Techniques of Improvisation," and Lawrence Koch's 1988 book, *Yardbird Suite: A Compendium of the Life and Music of Charlie Parker* (a greatly expanded version of articles he had published in two 1975 issues of *Journal of Jazz Studies*). Despite the fascinating musical issues raised by these studies, the proliferation of academic jazz studies programs, acceptance of jazz as a *bona fide* scholarly discipline, establishment of journals eager to publish jazz-related material, and the ongoing efforts of cultural custodians to define a jazz canon—the serious examination of Charlie Parker's music has languished until this book by Henry Martin.

Like other great music, Parker's has the potential for any number of different approaches to its analysis. His music is so well made and his techniques so concentrated and integrated that no single method seems a sufficient or best path to its understanding. Whereas Owens was chiefly concerned with the formulaic construction of Parker's melodic vocabulary and Koch (in the *Werk* portions of his *Leben und Werk* treatment) with the harmonic relationships of melody to a given chord pattern, Martin focuses on a kind of structural motivic organization that is revealed in a comparison of the basic linear design of Parker's improvised melodies with those of the thematic material he used.

Make no mistake about it: this is a serious and "technical" study. What sets it apart from much recent "technical" writing about jazz is the sensible and undoctrinaire way that Martin allows the music to suggest a hybrid voice-leading/motivic strategy for its analysis rather then imposing some well-rehearsed or currently-chic theory that is more celebrating of its applied methods than illumining the musical object of study. Despite a voluminous literature, most jazz scholarship remains in its infancy when compared to the intellectual standards that are taken for granted in the traditional areas of music history and theory. *Charlie Parker and Thematic Improvisation* is a giant leap forward, and Scarecrow Press should be commended for its wisdom in publishing it. Henry Martin has brought to this book the stuff that a serious examination of Charlie Parker's music deserves: a first-class mind, unflinching rigor, broad experience of and sensitivity to the music. While one might not concur with some of his arguments or "hear" all the connections his analyses demonstrate, the simple point is that Martin has established a new standard of discourse by which future musical studies of jazz will be measured.

JAMES PATRICK
STATE UNIVERSITY OF NEW YORK-BUFFALO

Acknowledgments

This book originates in a paper read at the 1992 national convention of the American Musicological Association in Pittsburgh. I would like to thank the AMS for the opportunity to present my work there.

A special word of thanks is in order to Dan Morgenstern and Ed Berger of the Institute of Jazz Studies at Rutgers University in Newark. Their enthusiasm for the original paper eventually led to an invitation to revise and enlarge it for publication in their *Studies in Jazz* series. Ed Berger gave a close reading to the final manuscript and contributed many useful comments. David Cayer was the copy editor and did a superb job.

Among other colleagues who read preliminary versions of the manuscript and made helpful suggestions were Bill Kirchner and Robert Sadin. Thanks to Bill who alerted me to a number of possible follow-up ideas regarding sources of melodic ideas. To Bob a very special thank you—both for comments on this book and for those unforgettable nuggets of wisdom on jazz, concert music, and culture both musically and sociologically. It's an intellectual and creative debt extending over many years that can never be acknowledged in full.

Especially close criticism by Barry Kernfeld, Fred Lerdahl and Jim Patrick were invaluable in producing the final version. Barry's running commentary on the historical and cultural material of an early draft was virtually a mini-paper in itself; many of his proposals and suggestions were incorporated. Fred suggested numerous adjustments and refinements to Ch. 2, so that the theoretical background is now both clearer and more exact.

Jim Patrick made excellent suggestions which resulted in improvements to the book's large-scale form and to the delineation of Parker's style more specifically. I am indebted, too, to his outstanding knowledge of Parker recordings, which forms the basis of the Ch. 1 footnote on statistics. Finally, a very special thanks to Jim for his gracious introduction.

Others I would like to thank who helped me in various ways to formulate the book and shape its contents: John Halsey, with whom I have spent much time discussing the implications of jazz and cultural history;

Gary Giddins for pointing out a possible melodic source of Parker's "Embraceable You" motive; Milton Babbitt for the intellectual stimulation of thinking about and knowing music as intimately as possible; and Gunther Schuller for inspiration in the broad appreciation of worthy music of all types, for his path-breaking writing about jazz, and for discussions on wide-ranging issues involving the theory of jazz and other forms of Western music.

Finally, I would especially like to thank Lewis Porter who functioned as editor of this volume. Lew's enthusiasm for the project helped make the book's possibility a reality. Lew gave generously—both of his time and of various borrowings from his impressive personal library. I am greatly indebted to him for taking such care on the book's many and varied stages—not only his careful scrutiny of the manuscript, but also his checking some of the music as presented in the transcriptions and analyses. Working with him was a pleasure in all phases of the project; I cannot conceive of an editor's function better fulfilled.

A final word of thanks is owed to my parents, Mary and Henry Martin, Sr., who have supported all my musical and intellectual endeavors with never-flagging enthusiasm. This book is dedicated to them.

We gratefully acknowledge permission to reprint the following songs. All companies hold international copyright and reserve all rights.

Au Privave, by Charlie Parker, © 1956, 1978 (renewed 1984) Atlantic Music Corp. Blues for Alice, by Charlie Parker, © 1956, 1978 (renewed 1984) Atlantic Music Corp. Bongo Bop, by Charlie Parker, © 1961 (renewed) Duchess Music Corp., an MCA company. Cherokee (Indian Love Song), words and music by Ray Noble, © 1938 The Peter Maurice Music Co. © renewed and assigned to Shapiro, Bernstein & Co. Cheryl, by Charlie Parker, © 1947 (renewed 1975), 1978 Atlantic Music Corp. Cool Blues (a/k/a/ Hot Blues [Cool Blues]), by Charlie Parker, © 1961 (renewed) Duchess Music Corp., an MCA company. Crazeology, music by Benny Harris, © 1946 (renewed 1974) Screen Gems–EMI Music Inc. Embraceable You, music and lyrics by George Gershwin and Ira Gershwin, © 1930 (renewed) WB Music Corp. Just Friends, by Sam Lewis and John Klenner, © 1931 (renewed) EMI Robbins Catalog Inc. Used by permission of Warner Bros. Publications. Koko, by Charlie Parker, © 1946 (renewed 1974) Atlantic Music Corp. Now's the Time, by Charlie Parker, © 1945 (renewed 1973), 1978 Atlantic Music Corp. Parker's Mood, by Charlie Parker, © 1948 (renewed 1976), 1978 Atlantic Music Corp. Perhaps, by Charlie Parker, © 1948 (renewed 1976), 1978 Atlantic Music Corp. Red Cross, by Charlie Parker, © 1945 (renewed 1973), 1978 Atlantic Music Corp. Shaw Nuff, by Charlie Parker and Dizzy Gillespie, © 1946 (renewed) Consolidated Music Publishers, a division of Music Sales Corp. (ASCAP) and Atlantic Music International; © 1948 (renewed 1976), 1978 Atlantic Music Corp. Star Eyes, by Don Raye and Gene De Paul, © 1943 (renewed) EMI Feist Catalog. Used by permission of Warner Bros. Publications. Thriving from a Riff, by Charlie Parker, © 1945 (renewed 1973), 1978 Atlantic Music Corp.

Chapter 1

Introduction

Formula and Thematic Improvisation

Charlie Parker's recorded legacy is imposing, often brilliant, and—perhaps like the work of great improvisers generally—startling in its unity. This unity becomes more apparent the more the recordings are played, replayed, compared, and contrasted: much of what we hear in one can be heard in others, but the disposition, the personality, changes. Similar ideas drift from performance to performance, but subtle changes keep them fresh: this is by no means shallow repetition or mechanical playing in the worst sense. Instead, we are struck by the essential mystery of Parker's greatness: how can a player who seems to duplicate ideas from solo to solo continue to be so musically satisfying? With ever-recurring melodic ideas permeating his mature work, it might seem odd that the recent and serendipitous discovery of surely less significant recordings, such as the Dean Benedetti tapes,[1] would generate as much interest as they have among Parker admirers. But all of Parker's work is important—despite the repetitions in his improvisational ideas, there seem to be new twists, new spins, new directions that continue to fascinate: we have heard this before, but not quite in the same way. We want to hear everything we can, and we do not tire of what we know well.

Previous large-scale studies[2] of Parker's music, rather than trying to analyze the particularities of his excellence, have concentrated instead on the generalities: what ideas are duplicated from solo to solo—these will be called "formulas" in this book—and when they are played, i. e., what kinds of melodic figures are likely to occur and in what harmonic-formal contexts are they to be found. Despite the useful insight into improvisational method, the elucidation of Parker "clichés" is benumbing; musical interest recedes upon analysis that principally shows that Parker played something close to this very phrase elsewhere in a similar context.

This study, on the other hand, attempts to discover why Parker's

2 Charlie Parker and Thematic Improvisation

music works so well despite the apparent reliance on formula, and, as a corollary, to investigate relationships between the improvisations and the original tunes,[3] or "heads." Among other things, I hope to show that formula is not synonymous with cliché—that the use of formula is necessary for competent improvisation. I especially hope to show that thematic relationships may exist even when Parker's playing seems indifferently connected to the original melody—and, further, that these sometimes hidden relationships may partly explain why Parker's music remains so compelling despite surface repetition. An important byproduct of the analysis is, simply, further insight into Parker's style and the ways of jazz improvisation more generally.[4]

While at first glance it may not seem unusual that a Parker improvisation should relate thematically to the melody that it is based on, this view is somewhat contrary to established opinion. The dominating theoretical work in this field has been Thomas Owens's "Charlie Parker: Techniques of Improvisation," an impressive and thorough study of about 250 improvisations in all of Parker's major genres. Owens concludes,

> In spontaneously composing, he [Parker] drew primarily on a repertory of about 100 motives of varying lengths, modifying them and combining them in a great variety of ways. Consequently, his solos are normally organized without reference to the theme of the piece being performed.[5]

Owens shows that Parker's style—especially in uptempo playing—is heavily dependent on these melodic formulas,[6] which reappear in various recombinations from solo to solo.

James Patrick, in the *New Grove Dictionary of Jazz*, confirms Owens's opinion:

> Parker's improvisations usually ignore the original melody, being based instead on its harmonic structure. Melodic ornamentation or paraphrase occasionally occurs, but characteristically these are reserved for thematic statements of popular melodies in the opening or closing chorus [example reference]. However, his use of rhythm and pitch is sometimes subtly linked to the pulse and the chord progressions of the original.[7]

Or again, Max Harrison:

> Indeed, at times Parker seemed to be a "pure" improviser, to whom the character and quality of the theme made little difference.[8]

That Parker indeed constructs his solos from a group of motivic formulas is uncontestable, especially in uptempo playing. What this study questions is Owens's claim, backed up by Patrick and Harrison, that Parker's solos "are normally organized without reference to the theme of the piece being performed."[9]

The analyses of Parker's solos presented in the chapters to follow suggest that Parker would often absorb the *underlying* foreground motives and voice-leading structures of the themes, then fashion his solos in light of that larger-scale thematic material.[10] That is, Parker connects to the source material through middleground voice leading, and by abstracting, internalizing, then projecting essential, if sometimes less evident, qualities of the head. It is highly probable that Parker did not plan or intend many, if any, of the relationships to be cited in the analyses to follow, yet if they can be demonstrated, his work—at its best unsurpassed as self-contained improvisation—is further enhanced through closer association with the original compositions.

My thesis will be argued through sample analyses drawn from three areas of his work: rhythm changes[11] in the key of B♭, popular standards, and the blues. Because of the apparent similarity of the solos (through the extensive use of improvisational formulas), but distinctiveness of the themes, this study begins with and devotes considerable space to Parker's rhythm-changes improvisations. The rhythm-changes model accounts for about 12 percent of Parker's recordings, second only to the blues which accounts for some 24 percent.[12] Moreover, B♭ major was Parker's preferred key for rhythm changes.[13] Hence, if Parker's numerous improvisations on rhythm changes in B♭ seem differentiable on the basis of the head, then the same might be surmised for his work more generally. After examining rhythm changes, the remainder of the analyses tests this hypothesis by checking Parker's work in his two other main improvisational genres, popular song and the blues.[14]

Regarding the general organization of this volume, issues in the techniques and methods of bebop analysis are discussed in Chapter 2, while Chapters 3–5 examine a sampling of Parker's improvisations. The final chapter sums up Parker's style, specifically with respect to formula and thematic reference. Then, rather as an addendum, the role of formula and literacy in orally-based art forms is touched upon, then applied to jazz history to help place jazz in general, and Parker in particular, within the tradition of Western culture. Finally, with these discussions and the previous analyses in mind, Parker's importance is evaluated in the context of music in our time.

It is conceded from the start that Parker, as a rule, does not consciously develop the original thematic material, say, in the paradigmatic sense of Beethoven in his sonata forms. Yet, to view Parker's solos as strings of interchangeable, or sometimes even redundant, melodic formulas implies that the heads are virtually unnecessary. My sense of this music is that a masterful Parker solo is far more than a sequence of thematically irrelevant formulas, linked to the original solely by harmony. Further, thematic connections would seem still more likely, since Parker's best solos usually contain genuinely surprising moments—at first hearing, anyway—which would be difficult to account for if all his solos within some genre were roughly equivalent. To attribute this effect to such generalities as variety in the "mix"[15] of his motivic formulas seems to vastly oversimplify the effect of perhaps the most sophisticated improvisation in jazz history.

In any event, thematic interconnection, if it exists, must be sought elsewhere than in conscious motivic development. The studies in this volume not only seek to show thematic interconnection at a more unconscious level, but also, where appropriate, invoke hierarchical voice-leading principles, since this route has been most promising for investigating less overt associations between solos and heads. I write "voice-leading" rather than, say, "Schenkerian" because Schenker[16] did not apply his techniques to jazz, and because my analytical method is based on the voice-leading and harmonic practices of bebop. More precisely, my analytical method consists of seeking relationships common to both head and solos, and which are referred to, in Ch. 2, as "thematic patterns," to choose as neutral a term as possible. These very general relationships *may* include features uncovered by voice-leading analysis, but are certainly not limited to such relationships.[17] Indeed, much of the analysis in this book is motivic and does not require close examination of the voice leading. What the latter method of analysis will confirm, however, is that Parker very carefully controls the voice-leading tendencies of his improvised lines; indeed, he typically projects three or four well-controlled voice-leading lines simultaneously.

A final note before proceeding: at first glance this book might be regarded as an attempt to prove Owens wrong. This is most emphatically not the case. As stated above, Owens demonstrates definitively Parker's typical reliance on motivic formulas, especially in uptempo playing. His conclusions are vitally important—they illustrate techniques that may be necessary for improvisational fluency. Nor has anyone gone to such lengths as Owens in cataloguing this essential element of jazz improvisation as it relates, more broadly, to the oral tradition in music. In this regard, his work is an important companion for more thematically-oriented analysis. I will argue in my concluding remarks that for improvising players such reliance on formulas can be expected — is even necessary — since thematic "redundancy" is required by the nature of oral expression. What is slighted in Owens's study is how Parker transcends the mechanical application of formulas; and how in many instances their effectiveness lies in unexpected motivic connection to the original thematic material. This book, then, is a corrective, a redistribution of the balance of Owens's assessment, not a demonstration of its invalidity.

Transcriptions

A word on transcriptions: since a jazz improvisation is not normally notated by the player who performed it, its transcription is an analytical statement — an interpretation of what was played, an analytical first stage, or a "reading" of the solo. A transcription acknowledges the analyst's point of view, reveals theoretical agenda, musical background — all the usual, but significant predispositions. Despite this caveat concerning transcription's essential relativity and distance from the artistic intent of the player, those included in this volume attempt to be as "honest" to what was played as is practical.

A common and often-discussed problem in "honestly" notating what was played is how to deal with chordal notation when there is harmonic disagreement among the players: just what *are* the changes that should be understood for purposes of analysis? The issue is complicated by a related series of difficulties, the first being that the original chord changes[18] of most tunes adopted by jazz players are usually modified in interpretation, with the modifications themselves often part of the arrangement. In some instances, the intended modifications may not even accord well with parts of the original melody.[19]

To complicate an already difficult situation, the accompanying chordal players — pianist or guitarist — often modify the harmonies while comping[20] with changes that may be ignored (or unnoticed) by the improvising soloist. Finally, the improvising soloist may also be playing in such a manner that the solo line implies yet further modifications of the harmonies, which may be ignored or unnoticed by the rhythm section.

The only realistic solution to this problem is that the analyst must make choices that seem reasonable for the purposes of the analysis, while being true to "what's there." In the analysis of chord changes as abstract entities, such as those introduced in the next section, "ideal" changes—those typically established in the head—work well: there is no given melody present to complicate the situation by clashing with the changes.

In uptempo improvisation, it is often impossible for the soloist and rhythm section to anticipate each other's spontaneous modifications or omissions of prevailing harmonies; hence, changes that remain close to the model established in the head will usually work well for purposes of notation. Further, the use of the implied harmonies of the head "smooths out" the problem of accompanists who omit chords: for example, (to cite just one typical instance) pianist Duke Jordan on "Crazeology," (Ch. 3, Ex. 3–8), consistently omits the D♭7 chord of the A♭m7-D♭7-G♭M7 chord pattern on Parker's solos, on all takes. He also rarely backs up the conclusions of Parker's choruses with cadences to a B♭M tonic. Yet, the basic, the understood, chord pattern is notated on the examples so that the harmonic flow, even if implied, remains clear. This kind of problem is typical of uptempo transcription.

At slower tempos, a more leisurely harmonic rhythm permits more spontaneous reaction among the players so that, as a result, a possibly more complicated harmonic scenario is relevant: the players can use what they hear before it passes by. Again, when useful, the more detailed chords heard will be noted on the transcriptions.

Often, too, it sounds as if Parker was virtually ignoring the harmonies as supplied by the rhythm section; nor might it be clear what changes Parker himself may have had in mind. In such instances, harmonic clashes may occur; nevertheless, the actual chords heard in the rhythm section will be notated, although they may not be relevant to Parker's line.

The preceding decisions are practical and only serve to clarify points in the analysis. To sum up, the actual chords played by the rhythm section will be notated, unless, in some uptempo improvisation, it is simpler to assume the "ideal" chords heard (or implied) in the head. By trying to show "what is there" as much as is realistic, readers can thereby make their own interpretations.

The transcriptions included in this volume are for analytical rather than pedagogical use, so they are notated in concert key. Phrasing, dynamics, and other forms of expression are excluded since they clutter the notation and do not add appreciably to the analytical points being made. The occasional exception will be accents, which are often relevant to the voice-leading implications of Parker's line. "Ghosted" notes—those played very softly or merely implied—are notated with "x" noteheads. Scoops, glissandi, and "fall-offs," will be notated with the customary lines and curves. For pitch notation, the system used denotes the octave from middle C to the B a seventh above as C4 to B4. The octave above middle C is C5-B5, the octave below is C3-B3, and so on. Bars will be numbered relative to sections in the form with a chorus number (if necessary) preceding. For example, m. 2A3-4 means the second chorus, third A section, fourth measure. In blues, a section number is unnecessary: m. 2-4 means second chorus, fourth measure. This method of numbering bars facilitates cross-comparisons between sections and choruses.

Finally, since transcriptions are interpretations and therefore inexact, they will often differ depending on the notator. In some instances, I base my view of what was played on previous transcriptions. Other times, despite the existence of previous work, I transcribed the passage myself. When previous transcriptions were consulted initially, they are acknowledged, despite occasional changes and emendations to bring them into line with what I heard on the recording.

Chapter 2

Improvisation and Linear Theory

Strophic Form and Harmonic Prolongation

Bop improvisation is based exclusively on strophes (called "choruses" in jazz) of usually 12 bars (the blues), or 16 and 32 bars (song forms with standard variants). The most common song forms are AABA or ABAC — typically 32 bars divided into 8-bar sections (with occasional extensions, tags, or other modifications). The large-scale strophic form of bop improvisation insures harmonic and formal closure at regular, predictable, and rather closely-spaced intervals. The formal closure of each individual strophe implies that the large-scale form of a multi-chorus solo is akin to the classical theme and variations model — a topic that will be discussed below.

For the most part, the harmonic plan in bop tunes[21] (or popular standards chosen or adapted for bop use) is straightforward: chord progressions are usually based on functional relationships derived from the circle of fifths. Examples 2–1 and 2–2[22] show that rhythm changes and the blues, typical vehicles for bop improvisation, project the tonic triad unambiguously through nested harmonic prolongations. The A section in rhythm changes consists of a "busy" I-VI-II-V pattern, but (as will be discussed below) is usually simplified. The blues consists of three four-bar phrases, each ending with the tonic for the final two chords: each phrase in effect approaches the final tonic uniquely, first through the I and V chords (first phrase), then the IV chord (second phrase), then a combination of V and IV (third phrase).

The *bridge* in rhythm changes (Ex. 2–1) prolongs the the large-scale tonic, or key of the piece, "by arrival." In prolongation "by arrival," the tonic of the piece is, in effect, constructed by a predictable succession of chords that sets up that tonic as the goal harmony of the end of the section.[23] Such progressions are common — being heard frequently in such pieces as "Autumn Leaves"[24] (Ex. 2–3), which arrives at E minor as the

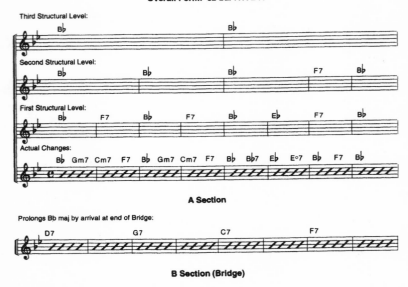

Ex. 2-1: Rhythm Changes

Overall Form: 32-bar A A B A

A Section

B Section (Bridge)

tonic of the initial 8-bar A section. Notice that the E-minor harmony, though clearly the tonic, is not articulated earlier in the changes—instead the circle-of-fifths progression *through* E-minor harmonies and the predictable 8-bar timespan together serve to delineate the function of the tonic. Arrival-at-the-tonic forms of progression are also found in songs associated with earlier jazz styles, such as "Sweet Georgia Brown"[25] or "Jazz Me Blues."[26] The bridge of rhythm changes (Ex. 2–1) functions similarly in its return to the tonic at the beginning of the A section.

Harmonic structure in bop style, at both the small and large scale, tends to remain unambiguous throughout most of the repertory, even on those rare occasions when a single tonal center is not projected throughout a given piece. For example, the changes for "Giant Steps," arguably in late bop style, oscillate intriguingly among B, G and E♭ major tonal centers (Ex. 2–4). For that reason, this tune can be considered non-tonal, since it does not project a single key throughout. In fact, only level b, the first to be derived from the changes, is functionally based; levels c and d are suggested by analogy to the concept of arrival prolongation at the end

Ex. 2-2: Standard Blues

of customary timespans. That is, it is possible that significant departure or arrival points within predictable timespans can "prolong" the beginning or ending harmonies even if the changes are *not* always based on the circle of fifths. These speculative levels (c and d) could also be continued to even longer timespans until an E♭maj7 is reached as a "tonic," since it ends the piece. Still, rather than force some unique tonic for "Giant Steps," we ought instead recognize the tune's essential tonal ambiguity: the B, G and E♭ major "tonics" are the "giant steps" heard at a higher level of structure.

Notice also that in "Giant Steps," the harmonic rhythm halves in the second half of the tune, so that in one sense a level is skipped there: that is, in the second half, the harmonic rhythm relaxes, with II-V-I progressions

Ex. 2-3: Autumn Leaves (A Section)

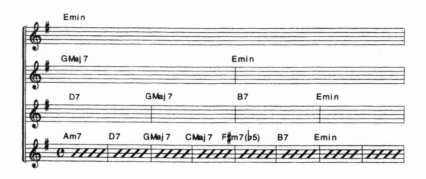

Ex. 2-4: Giant Steps

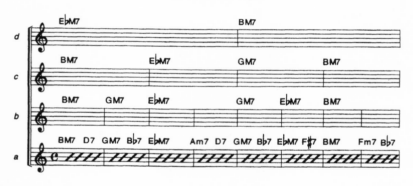

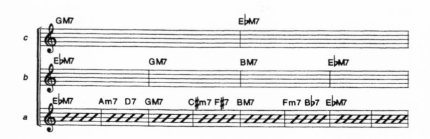

effected every *two* bars, whereas the first half of the piece is characterized by 1-bar prolongations. The complexity of "Giant Steps" is not typical of bop harmony in general,[27] but the example is included to show how the principles of bop harmony may be extended without endangering coherence.

Bop tunes will usually maintain harmonic and formal clarity in order to provide a solid large-scale basis for improvisation. Since the progression of the changes can be easily internalized, and the symmetry and regularity of the strophes "felt" without too much conscious attention, the player can focus on developing the melodic and expressive essence of a solo with these "built-in" formal factors taken for granted. Further, the harmonic and formal clarity of bop provides a framework for meaningful voice leading, both small- and large-scale, as will be discussed in the next two sections.

Voice-leading Models

In any tonal style harmonic function is articulated through the presence or absence of voice leading. For example, overly attentive voice leading in the European fine-art tradition can contradict the tenets of a highly vernacular style, such as heavy metal. Voice-leading analysis yields fruitful insights when adapted to bop.[28] It can uncover unexpected musical detail and track the overall flow of an improvisation in much the same way as traditional voice-leading analysis of European common-practice music. This is because solo lines and melodies in bop style articulate functional changes, such as those analyzed in the previous section; they are "melodically fluent,"[29] that is, based on the traditional Western concept of normative stepwise motion between chord changes. Hence, voice-leading analysis reveals important insights into how the changes are negotiated by the player. Charlie Parker's skill as an improviser derives in part from his superb voice leading.[30]

Voice-leading analysis is rather more straightforward in bop than in tonal concert music, since the improvisations tend to be entirely melodic rather than multi-voice. Even bop pianists concentrate on single-line melody. With the complications of fully-developed, multi-part jazz composition mostly avoided in practice, such complex and controversial issues of traditional Schenkerian theory as the status of structural levels over long time-spans, to cite one example, rarely arise: the music remains melodically concentrated and rather circumscribed formally. Further,

given bop's chromatism, nondiatonic fundamental lines and other devi-
ations from Schenkerian orthodoxy occur with frequency. Thus there is
no *required* descent of a diatonic fundamental line from $\hat{3}$, $\hat{5}$ or $\hat{8}$.

The preceding section of this chapter showed the relative ease with
which chord changes—as given entities without any music interpreting
them—can be analyzed hierarchically. Analyzing the voice-leading implications of actual bop melodic lines requires an understanding of relative
consonance and dissonance in relation to the underlying harmonic changes.
More fundamentally, tonal theory views increasing consonance as indica-
tive of greater structural import, with perhaps the most fundamental
distinction being the chord versus nonchord tone. In bop melodic lines,
passing and neighbor tones, as the most familiar nonchord tones from standard tonal theory, are ubiquitous and should be understood as structurally
dependent on the chord tones they connect. Suspensions, anticipations and
appoggiaturas also occur, with suspensions treated freely for the most part:
they are rarely prepared and resolved as in common-practice theory.

An important deviation from common-practice tonal theory is the existence in bop of "extended-chord tones" (sevenths, ninths, elevenths,
thirteenths, and their chromatic alterations), which may function either
as chord tones or nonchord tones. In either case they are relatively dissonant to the pitches of the underlying triad. Such extended-chord tones
have been called "tensions" in order to emphasize their structural de-
pendence on the more fundamental triadic tones:

> In a tonal diatonic setting, a tension is a pitch related to a struc-
> turally superior pitch (usually a chord tone) by step, such that the
> tension represents and substitutes for the structurally superior
> pitch, called its resolution, in the register in which it occurs. Most
> tensions are located a step above their resolutions. The concept of
> tension is broader than that of suspension, appoggiatura, passing
> tone, or neighbor tone, as there is no requirement of manner of ap-
> proach, manner of leaving, or rhythmic position in its definition.[31]

Analysis of small-scale voice leading in bop thus proceeds along lines
established in general tonal theory: nonchord tones, such as passing
tones, neighbors (both complete and incomplete), suspensions, anticipations and appoggiaturas function similarly. In addition, there will be
found a broader category of extended-chord tones that are structurally
dependent on the more fundamental triadic pitches, but sometimes may
be treated as harmonic qualities of the underlying chord itself. More
specifically: if the extended-chord tones resolve to triadic pitches before

the harmony changes, then they usually function as standard nonchord tones (passing tones, neighboring tones, etc.). As such they tend to resolve downwards, but as is the case with nonchord tones in common-practice music, upwards resolutions are also common. When extended-chord tones do not resolve within the prevailing harmony, they may impart their intrinsic quality to the underlying chord and may even be prolonged at higher levels of structure, as will be shown in the next section.

To compare bop style to the common-practice style favored traditionally by voice-leading analysis, let us examine the opening of Bach's *Partita in D Minor* for solo violin. In the excerpt given in Ex. 2–5, a complete harmonic statement prolongs the tonic triad. As the top staff in the analysis shows, three or four voice-leading lines are projected. The A4 in m. 1 arises from an unfolded tonic triad. Let us label as Q the unfolded third, F4-A4, the third and fifth of the tonic triad. Prolonged briefly by a B♭4 neighbor on the last 16th note of the second beat, the A4 is then prolonged through to the triplet 16ths at the end of m. 2. Within this prolongation of A4 from m. 1, "and" of beat 2, to m. 2, beat 4, there are two internal occurrences of Q. The second of these is interrupted by a tritone skip to C♯4 from the second to the third beat of m. 2.

The G4 at the end of the second beat of m. 2 can also be thought of as a displaced G3 (given in parentheses), which would complete a pattern of rising seconds (in m. 2) connecting to bass pitches: C♯4-D4, A3-B♭3, then "G3"-A3. This interpretation also mitigates the parallel fifths connecting B♭3-F4 to A3-E4 from the second to the third beat of m. 2.

Within the unfolded-third framework provided by motive Q, the subtlety of the third and fourth beats of m. 1 can be placed in relief. Although A4 is the prolonged pitch in the top voice, B♭4 is the pitch slightly accented by virtue of its being skipped to and from the intervening C♯4 on

Ex. 2-5: Bach Partita in D Minor for Violin

the third beat. The same pattern is repeated on the fourth beat, where the G4 is accented by the intervening skip to E5. And, of course, the C#4 and E5 are also accented through their registral and metrical placement as well as being the pitches skipped *to* in each case. Hence, while a dominant triad in first inversion is the harmony to be inferred on the third and fourth beats, the more prominently accented pitches strongly imply the more dissonant C#dim 7th chord (VII dim 7) as well.

The harmonic ambiguity of the third and fourth beats of m. 1 prepares us for the beauty of Bach's placement of the G4 on the last 16th of m. 2, beat 2. The skip away from G4 to the C#4 parallels the dissonant skip to that pitch heard in m. 1 and again subtly accents the G4. The interruption of motive Q at this point creates, in effect, a subtle syncopation of the G4, and parallels the syncopation of B♭4 and G4 as the last 16ths of the second and third beats of m. 1.

The statement of motive Q on the triplet 16ths that complete m. 2 provides a wonderful culmination of the phrase: after Q's greatest disruption (at the end of the second beat of m. 2), we now hear Q stated evenly for the first time since m. 1, beat 2. That is, for Q's first appearance, the A4, G4, and F4 were consecutive 16ths; at the end of the phrase they all placed regularly on 8th beats. (This is visually apparent by just comparing the layout of the four instances of motive Q on the top staff.)

Thus an apparently simple prolongation of the tonic triad disguises some rather complex syncopations of important pitches as well as finely wrought motivic continuity. Most importantly for our purposes, Bach is able to project three, sometimes four, voice-leading lines monophonically with surprising syncopations of key pitches en route. This virtual syncopation of the voice leading is also very common in bop. As will become evident in the analyses to follow, bop lines in general — and Parker's lines in particular — project a flow of harmonic changes and motivic continuity in very similar fashion.

Example 2–6 shows the voice leading of the Bach excerpt broken down into suggested individual voice-leading "parts" and placed in relief against the background meter. Each part centers around and describes the immediate voice-leading environment of the prolonged D-minor tonic triad. Here, the nonrhythmic quality of the analysis seen in Ex. 2–5 is animated vividly by hearing the de facto syncopation of the voice leading contrasted with the regularity and evenness of the sixteenth-note motion. Each part, taken alone, proceeds in irregular fashion with resulting syncopations, though the actual melody, the aggregate perception of the voice leading, is smooth. The registrally prominent top part in staff a

Ex. 2-6: Bach Partita "Parts"

converges rhythmically to the A4 on the fourth beat of m. 2 — where motive Q ends the phrase — so that the A4's earlier articulation of 8th beats can be heard as preparing the pitch's climactic appearance *on* the beat.

The unraveling of the "parts" demonstrated in Ex. 2–6 provides much voice-leading insight, but can obscure motivic connections — the kind shown in Ex. 2–5. Still, the exercise does illustrate how monophonic lines are able to project harmonically sophisticated counterpoint with unexpected twists of syncopation. The parts themselves will tend to center around the pitches of the tonic triad or whatever harmony is currently prolonged. Since passing motions will connect some tonic-triad pitches to others, discrete voice-leading lines will appear and disappear depending on the direction of the monophonic line and the range it covers. Parker is like Bach in that projection of three or four voice-leading parts tends to be the norm, as will be seen in the following example.

The excerpt in Ex. 2–7 is from Parker's solo on "Shaw 'Nuff,"[32] just before the bridge, and, as in the Bach excerpt, presents a complete harmonic statement prolonging the tonic triad. The analysis shows Parker navigating the changes with similar precision: the melody is fluent, with no pitches "left hanging," that is, unaccounted for in the voice leading. To put it more precisely, while the changes progress harmonically to B♭ major, all the pitches in the melody not included in the B♭ triad proceed to their expected resolutions at the arrival of the tonic.

While a composed-out third unifies the Bach excerpt (Ex. 2–5), a large-scale neighbor motion provides the basis for the Parker example.

Ex. 2-7: Parker "Shaw 'Nuff" Excerpt

The fundamental neighbor motion is itself syncopated: the D4 on the downbeat of m. 1 proceeds to E♭4 on the downbeat of m. 2. Given the regular harmonic rhythm that returns to B♭ major on the downbeat of m. 3, we might expect Parker to articulate D4 on that downbeat as well. Instead a C4 appears at m. 3 and the D4 is delayed to the "and" of the second beat. This syncopation of the motion, playing off against the regularity of the harmonic rhythm, is typical of bop melodic lines, especially Parker's.

The interpretation of the G4 on the fourth beat of m. 1 is ambiguous and shows the subtlety with which Parker reinforces the large-scale neighbor motion. For within the context of a B♭7 chord, one might at first read the G4 as a simple appoggiatura to the more stable chord tone F4. Yet, three factors suggest that the G4 can also be read as a large-scale upper neighbor connecting back to the F4 as the pick-up to m. 1: the speed of the excerpt, the analogous position of G4-E♭4 with the F4-D4 third beginning the phrase, and the accent on the G4 itself. The motion to the E♭ harmony of m. 2 is thus anticipated (syncopated) by a beat. In effect, the G4 can be considered a 13th of the dominant chord, which, according to standard usage in bop, anticipates the third of the following tonic. (The 13th of the dominant may also resolve directly to the Î supported by the tonic triad.) The G4-F4-E♭4 line from beat four of m. 1 to the downbeat of m. 2 thus transposes and composes out more slowly the F4-D4 third beginning the excerpt.

The C♯4 in m. 2 reinforces the neighbor idea with a lower neighbor to the final D4; thus the D4 is encircled by a double-neighbor motion. The C4 on the downbeat of m. 3 interrupts the resolution of C♯4 to D4 with an appoggiatura to B♭3, thus enabling the syncopation of the final D4.

Against the swirl of neighbor motions, resolutions, and syncopations

surrounding the principal pitches D4 and F4, Parker also manages to fit in
a bass line of B♭3, A♭3, and G3. An especially effective quality of this line
is the delay of the G3 after the rapid syncopation of B♭3 and A♭3. This delay parallels the delay of the resolution of C♯4 in m. 2 to the D4 in m. 3.

Thus Parker projects three or four voice-leading lines which articulate
the changes in a manner akin to the Bach excerpt in Ex. 2–5 and 2–6.
Further, as shown in Ex. 2–8, each voice-leading "part" proceeds irreg-
ularly against the meter and the perceived evenness of the eighth-note
line—again, in a manner quite similar to the Bach excerpt. Staves a and
b show the syncopated neighbor motion of D4-F4 to E♭4-G4 that is germane to the structure of the solo itself (as described in the next section
and in the more extended analysis of Ch. 3). By mentally projecting the
voice-leading sketch with each part distinguished against the metric regularity, the listener can hear the analysis in real time, where the complexity of the compound melodic line is placed in clear relief.

Again, as in the Bach example, tonic-triad pitches anchor each of the
contrapuntal parts, with neighbor motions within parts, and passing motions as connectors. It is an analytical judgment just how to separate the
voices—when lines begin, end, and merge—but this is itself a hallmark
of a sophisticated contrapuntal style, which can resist too much codifi-
cation.

This complex of voice leading contributes to Parker's sense of swing,

Ex. 2-8: Parker "Shaw 'Nuff" "Parts"

since strong forward motion is created by the uneven temporal progression of the parts, and by Parker's unexpected accents that cause the ear to attend to each part in turn. Thus the multi-part line along with Parker's performance of it—his accents, ghosted notes, and subtle playing behind or ahead of the beat—creates his outstanding rhythmic drive and sense of propulsion.[33]

Larger-scale Structure and Thematic Patterns

The voice-leading analyses seen in the Bach and Parker examples of the previous section directly reveal the polyphonal structure of their compound melodies relative to the underlying harmonies, and, as such, are reasonably free of interpretive ambiguity. In one sense, it would be convenient to claim that because the foreground-based examples of the preceding section *do* seem reasonably straightforward, then all that is necessary is to continue the "same" process of discovering and depicting voice-leading fluency through higher levels of structures.

But voice leading does not work so conveniently in practice. Analyzing an already-derived musical level into an even more abstract background is not identical to deriving a foreground based on chord-to-chord connection. The criteria for a pitch to be "advanced" to a more background level are unclear. The consonance-dissonance requirement that often suffices at the foreground is simply impossible to apply unarbitrarily to higher levels where evidence of "support" is more equivocal. In practice, what the analyst tends to do is derive the higher levels by invoking (1) correspondences with the foreground (diminution), (2) completion of implied patterns, and (most vaguely) (3) the prominence or importance of the favored pitches through repetition, accent, or registral placement. These can be very subjective criteria.

The difficulty of deriving larger-scale levels of bop melodic lines is manifested by comparing the chord-changes discussion seen in the first section of this chapter with actual voice-leading analysis. In the former, the nesting structure of the changes is quite straightforward: it is clear how to move to a higher level of structure. With actual music, the harmonic and linear functions of the notes themselves create a *natural* complexity in which there is no unambiguous method of promoting some given note to a higher level of structure—that is, in agreed-upon and musically appealing ways. Even at the foreground, as was seen in the preceding section, there are questions about which pitches are structurally superior. Voice-leading analysis is in fact a skill, a talent to be developed, in which the analyst, selecting among numerous possibilities, settles on those which drive home a specific point of view.

It is not pertinent to this study to examine in detail the ever-growing literature on voice-leading analysis from Schenker to the present, but some attention to these issues and other aspects of large-scale structure is in order, since such interpretations are occasionally posited in the analyses to follow. Indeed, higher-level interpretations, credibly derived from such foreground analysis as seen in the Bach and Parker examples of the previous section, can reveal the overall progress of individual pieces. For the power of voice-leading analysis lies in its advocacy of harmony as primary in large-scale tonal progressions: it shows how tonal compositions are unified through nested harmonic structures, and how these may be related to foreground detail.

More precisely, in tonal compositions, harmony (i. e., the voice-leading implications of the pitches that are conceptualized as "harmony") is built up hierarchically through the interlocking of voice-leading lines, whose interaction results in prolongation at increasingly larger-scale levels. Such emphasis is especially promising for the analysis of bop, since the harmonic focus of voice-leading analysis accords well with the circle-of-fifths functionality of bop-style changes. Most importantly, the task of positing larger-scale structures in bop analysis is rendered simpler for two principal reasons: its harmonic clarity and use of small strophic forms, which keeps most of the analysis close to the foreground. Higher-level analyses of bop strophes in fact resemble the intermediate levels of longer, more fully developed concert compositions.

It is particularly significant in bop style that extended-chord tones, or tensions, may be prolonged beyond their immediate harmonic environment—that is, these pitches *can* acquire greater structural status in bop, although their dissonance relative to the underlying triad remains. Sevenths in particular can function as consonances not requiring any further resolution.[34] As described above, extended-chord tones beyond the seventh are often resolved at the level of the chord changes, and generally are seen as clearly subordinate to the more conventional triadic pitches.

The promotion of extended-chord tones to higher levels of structure can be seen in Ex. 2–9, the bridge to the head of "Shaw 'Nuff." The pitch A♭4 begins the bridge, coming off of a pick-up bar centering around D5. This pitch, the ♯11 of a D7(♭9)(♯11) chord, does not resolve to A4 or F♯4, the closest triad pitches, but is instead transferred to A♭5, which itself

Ex. 2-9: Shaw 'Nuff (Bridge Melody)

does not proceed immediately to a triadic pitch. Meanwhile, a Db5 enters in m. B-2, which continues the extended-chord harmonic idea: it is the #11 of a G7(b9)(#11) chord. This latter chord, since it includes a b9 extension, continues to support the Ab5 harmonically although the pitch is no longer present in the melody. Finally, the Ab5 is resolved in m. B-5, as a C7(#11)(13) chord enters supporting an A5. The A5 is a member of the F triad (V), and may be heard as proceeding to F5 in m. B-7. So the relatively dissonant Ab4 first heard in m. B-1 eventually yields to the diatonic A5 as the third of the V chord, but the progression is higher-level since it comprises four bars with a change of harmony and an octave transfer.

Another point to be noticed in Ex. 2–9 is that despite the prominence of the extended-chord tones, the voice leading eventually *does* converge to the tonic triad: 3̂ and 5̂ (D5 and F5) in Bb major. This will be seen as typical of Parker's style, both compositionally and improvisationally; dissonances may be prominantly articulated and prolonged temporally, but they are usually resolved, generally within the 8-bar section in which they are first heard.

A special example of a pitch which is dissonant according to European tonality, but can acquire higher-level status in a jazz-blues context is the blue third, or B3̂. The blue third is well known for its unstable status: it may be articulated as b3̂ or as a pitch between 3̂ and b3̂, and is often given a sliding intonation in performance. Pianists often strike the 3̂ and b3̂ together, or the $\hat{2}$ and $\flat\hat{3}$, to simulate the "blue" frequencies unobtainable on a piano. Hence the label B$\hat{3}$: the actual "pitch" of the third may not be defined by the equal-tempered system and thus resists denotation by conventional scale degrees.

Example 2–10, from Parker's solo on the second take of "Red Cross,"[35] shows how the B$\hat{3}$ may acquire higher-level status in a voice-leading analysis. The manner in which Parker articulates the D5 at m. A2-1 is part of a blues-like figure that can be heard as encompassing the sliding D♭5 at the end of the same bar. Rather than conceptualizing these pitches as separate at a higher level, it seems preferable to join them into a single blue third, which the analysis posits as a primary tone[36] to the entire solo (Ch. 3, Ex. 3-2). Despite the higher-level status thus accorded the B$\hat{3}$, at the foreground it can be heard as proceeding through C5 to B♭4 in m. A2-3. This small-scale resolution of the blue third, however, falls within a very fast double-time figure; the initial B$\hat{3}$ derives much of its force and higher-level status from its registral isolation relative to the first half of the solo. Since the solo does not fully resolve to $\hat{1}$ until m. A3-8, it seems reasonable to hear the fundamental line as proceeding from this B$\hat{3}$. The highest level of this solo is thus quite comparable to a Schenkerian *Ursatz*.

Ex. 2-10: Red Cross - Take 2 (Section A2)

Another important concept, central to the basic thesis of this study of Parker's music, is that higher-level structures, such as those examined in the preceding two examples, can be *thematic*—that is connected tellingly to the work at hand—even though such structures are less determinate or characteristic of the composition than lower-level structures. The same higher-level structures may recur from piece to piece, but it is *how* they recur that is significant. Higher-level structures in voice-leading analysis are usually of two types: step-wise progressions through an interval and neighbor motions. (Less often, perhaps, arpeggiation can be motivic as well.)

An example of higher-level motivic structure in a melody that reappears in an improvisation occurs in Parker's "Shaw 'Nuff." In Ex. 2–11, the second A section of the original melody is given. Throughout this section D5 is prolonged by neighbor motion to Eb5, such as in m. A2-3 and m. A2-5, so that this neighbor motion thereby assumes a thematic role in the section. Indeed, the importance of the neighbor motion is summed up in the final measure of the section, m. A2-8, where it appears twice in diminution.

The prolongation of D5 by neighbor motion to Eb5 is a *thematic pattern* of the original melody of "Shaw 'Nuff." It is not as characteristic, (or "determinate" or "thematic") of the original melody at the foreground as another motive, D5-F5 (the melody's first two pitches, labeled M in the discussion of "Shaw 'Nuff" in Ch. 3, Ex. 3–3), but it is of unquestionable import in the overall construction of the melody. Cadwallader and Pastille (1992) call this a "higher-level motive."[37] The more general term "thematic pattern" includes motives, both lower- and higher-level, and other aspects of melodic construction: groups of notes can be considered thematic patterns in melodies if they can be shown to be structurally significant in some convincing manner. This very general idea

Ex. 2-11: Shaw 'Nuff - Second A Section

will be elaborated on in the next section, when other types of thematic patterns are enumerated.

It was shown in Ex. 2–7 that Parker, in his solo on "Shaw 'Nuff," also elaborates a D-E♭-D neighbor motive in much the same way as in the head, though transposed down an octave. This same neighbor motion, D5-E♭5-D5, reappears significantly in the bridge of Parker's solo in its original register (Ex. 2–12). The pitch D5 has been prolonged from the earlier portion of the solo; in m. B-1 the pitch proceeds to E♭5 as a neighbor which is then prolonged as two dominant-seventh chord extensions—first the flat 9 of D7, then the flat 13 of G7—until m. B-5, when the D5 returns. Note also that this is another instance of a higher-level prolongation of an extended-chord tone.

Hence Parker's solo connects to the original melody of "Shaw 'Nuff" by duplicating one of its thematic patterns—in this instance, a higher-level motive of the original melody's A section which then reappears in the head and bridge of the solo—also as a higher-level motive. The D5-E♭5-D5 as a neighbor motion in the original melody is not a "motive" according to standard usage, but it is not merely a function of the piece's harmony either; other melodies on rhythm changes do not necessarily feature this motion as one of its characteristics. As Cadwallader and Pastille argue,[38] such higher-level motives are less determinate or characteristic of the music, but they still contribute thematically to its structure and are not merely a

Ex. 2-12: Shaw 'Nuff - Solo Bridge

byproduct or coincidental result of harmonic motion or the intrinsic nature of the tonal system. The higher the background status of such motives, the more likely they will recur in other works—but this does not mean that they are irrelevant thematically to the work at hand. Even the *Ursatz*, the original Schenkerian designation of the highest level of voice-leading structure in a given piece, influences the course of the work thematically, but far less determinately than a lower-level motive. The following discussion presents reasoning that backs up this point of view.

The linear function of a pitch is often equated with its melodic role and is thereby less conceptual than its harmonic function. For example, numerous arrangements and doublings of C, E, and G in various registers can be made to imply a C major harmony, but randomly changing the register of even a single note in a melody can distort it irrevocably. Hence linear quality is "closer" to the note itself—tied more intimately to the note's identity *qua* note—as opposed to harmonic function, which can often[39] be represented by other pitches of the same name (i. e., of the same pitch class). Since linear quality is more specific to a given melody, it is more thematic or motivic.

Because a melody heard in bop-style improvisation will usually project a single tonality over the course of the piece, its pitches take on harmonic function relative to their status as chord tones in the hierarchy of the changes: the higher the level a chord change appears in a harmonic analysis (such as in the examples given in the first section), the more the chord tones within that chord change are imbued with harmonic function and can serve as candidates for more background pitches. In traditional Schenkerian terms, such pitches can be considered as receiving more "support," although the term assumes a rather different status in jazz where support derives from chord changes (abstractions) that can be realized through comping in an infinite number of ways.[40]

On the other hand, the pitches in a melody can be thought of as having more linear function the more they participate in the motivic patterns that particularize the melody. It is in this sense that linear function is correctly thought to be "more thematic" than harmonic function. As pointed out above, linear function can be synonymous with the thematic aspects of a melody—indeed, linear qualities are what we think of *as* specifying or particularizing melody.

But while linear and harmonic function may sometimes be antithetical, they do not necessarily cancel each other out. For example, the final tonic of a melody will usually bear considerable harmonic *and* linear function. To substitute some other pitch, or merely to change its register, may satisfy the sense of harmonic closure, but distort the composition melodically.

Sometimes, nonchord tones are often thought to be devoid of harmonic function. But this is surely not the case, either: the choice of a chromatic or nonchromatic form of a dissonant passing tone, for example, is usually based on harmonic considerations.

All pitches in a tonal melody, therefore, are imbued with both linear and harmonic function to varying degrees—hence all pitches on all structural levels can be (to some extent) motivic. But the "closer" to the foreground, the more determinately linear is the pitch, therefore the more its motivic qualities are specific to the work at hand.

Voice-leading analysis, as shown in the Parker example above, is primarily harmonic, but not entirely.[41] Hence voice-leading analyses on a variety of levels can reveal motivic aspects of the music not otherwise evident. Because these concepts are ultimately inexact, it is quite impossible to particularize the meaning of "linear" and "harmonic" further except to note that by elevating a pitch to a more background level in a voice-leading analysis, the analyst is positing the pitch to be "more harmonic"—perhaps "more structural" in the harmonic sense—than pitches appearing only at more foreground levels.

A voice-leading analysis, therefore—often thought of as "athematic"—will posit some linear, hence some (potentially) thematic function, because all notes so represented *necessarily* project both linear and harmonic function. Again, this is because the prolongation of events—single pitches or melodic progressions through various intervals—must have *some* linear component. The extent to which pitches in voice-leading analyses reflect linear qualities is the extent to which they can function thematically. Harmonic progression may be underscored by voice-leading connections and the appearance of pitches at more background levels, but linear function is not thereby negated. In particular, unexpected linear qualities of a melody, insofar as they are not dependent on rhythm, can be disclosed by voice-leading analysis, as seen above in the Parker "Shaw 'Nuff" example. These linear qualities can have thematic-motivic ramifications. Ways in which this occurs—through thematic patterns—are described in the next section.

To summarize the foregoing argument:

(1) Pieces are characterized by thematic patterns, which include higher- and lower-level motives as well as other relationships (enumerated in the next section).

(2) The more foreground (lower-level) a thematic pattern, the more determinate or characteristic it is of the piece at hand. The more background (higher-level) the relationship, the more it is likely to be duplicated in other pieces.

(3) All pitches in a given piece possess linear and harmonic function, despite the level at which they occur.

(4) The placement of a pitch at a higher voice-leading level means that the analyst considers it to have greater harmonic-structural function, but this judgment does not negate entirely the pitch's linear function, or its interaction linearly, especially with other pitches occurring at that level.

(5) Therefore, higher analytical levels may disclose motivic relations—although the more foreground a motive is, the more it is likely to be uniquely characteristic of the work at hand.

Thematic patterns, when sufficiently large-scale, can include variants on traditional Schenkerian *Ursatz* forms. The key aspect of the *Ursatz*, as defined by Schenker,[42] is the establishment of a tonic, its prolongation through to a structural dominant, and final cadence back to the tonic. The structural dominant and its progression to the tonic establishes the key of the piece—especially if an initial tonic is lacking (which often happens in jazz and popular music)—and the $\hat{1}$ of the fundamental line.

Among the large-scale forms heard in the bop repertoire[43] most frequently are $\hat{3}$-$\hat{1}$ forms, $\hat{5}$-($\hat{4}$)-$\hat{3}$-$\hat{1}$ forms and blues forms, such as B$\hat{3}$-$\hat{1}$. Background forms common in bop are summarized in Ex. 2–13. The use of the melodic 13th over the structural dominant in resolution to the final $\hat{1}$ (Ex. 2–13a) is a common alteration of the standard Schenkerian $\hat{2}$/V-to-$\hat{1}$/I structural cadence. The $\hat{3}$-$\hat{1}$ form is quite common, therefore, as is its blue form B$\hat{3}$-$\hat{1}$ (Ex. 2–13b), a special jazz- and blues-oriented structure discussed above in Ex. 2–10.[44] Note that the salient feature of these backgrounds is their omission of the $\hat{2}$—instead some form of $\hat{3}$ is retained as a large-scale suspension becoming a 13th supported by the structural dominant before resolution to the tonic.

A background proceeding from $\hat{5}$ as a primary tone (Ex. 2–13c) can also be heard. As in backgrounds heard in the European repertoire, support for the $\hat{4}$ is often weak. For example, in "Embraceable You" (Ch. 4, Ex. 4–1), the first half proceeds from $\hat{5}$ to $\hat{3}$ without intervening $\hat{4}$—in the second half, $\hat{4}$ is present. As with backgrounds from $\hat{3}$, the $\hat{2}$ is often omitted in backgrounds from $\hat{5}$. Irregular backgrounds that conform to none of these archetypes appear from time to time, especially in tunes that de-

Ex. 2-13: Common Bop Background Forms

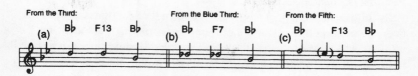

viate from tonal norms; this is certainly the case in "Giant Steps," for example.[45] Otherwise, large-scale voice-leading structures may not reveal *any* background form based on the models in Ex. 2–13, simply because at the highest level there may not be convincing support for some form of primary tone, the key feature for positing a fundamental line.

The backgrounds given in Ex. 2–13 are shown with the 13 or ♭13 supported by the structural dominant, but the usual Schenkerian forms that include the 2̂ supported by the structural dominant are also possible. Further, interrupted forms[46] very frequently occur with jazz- or popular-tune correlates. The ABAC song, with its half cadence at the end of the B section, frequently will imply an interrupted form, as can be seen in "Embraceable You" or "Just Friends" in Ch. 4.

Further variants of the backgrounds given in Ex. 2–13 will be heard in pieces that begin without establishing a tonic. In such instances, prolongation of the tonic by arrival establishes the key of the piece in question, although when initial tonics are not present, there is generally no convincing large-scale form. This is because large-scale forms must include a primary tone that must be given clear support from the tonic. Lack of an initial prolonged tonic in the changes precludes this possibility. For example, consider the "Autumn Leaves" A section (second time through), given in Ex. 2–14a: the descent from C5 to G4 is the primary voice-leading motion of the tune. The first time through the A section, the G4 is sustained; the second time through the A section, the G4 cadences to E4. Without an initial E minor tonic, it seems useless to posit some kind of background form beyond this foreground voice-leading line, for what could serve as the primary tone?

Alternatively, a kind of background *can* be found for "Autumn Leaves": although E minor as a tonic only arrives at the end of the A section, the tune itself is performed strophically—hence before each A section begins, the tune itself has already established E minor as the tonic. Further, the first time the A section is heard, it was probably preceded by an introduction that established E minor. The pick-up to the A section would be played over that E-minor tonic, and that pick-up includes a G4, which credibly serves as a primary tone for a background. This alternative analysis can be seen in Ex. 2–14b.

Despite the discovery of a background form for "Autumn Leaves," the main point should be clear—there are times in which standard backgrounds will not arise naturally from the voice leading in bop tunes or improvisations. In such cases, the analysis should not be forced—the more foreground voice-leading levels will provide the best picture of the overall direction of the piece. These and similar points will be amplified in the upcoming analyses when appropriate.

A final topic pertinent to this discussion of voice-leading issues in bop is the extent to which conceiving of background forms can be helpful in unifying multi-chorus—and thereby often fragmented—solos convincingly. Multi-chorus form in jazz is closely related to theme and variation form in European music, where strophes are delineated by harmonic and thematic interior cadences. Whereas jazz musicians will sometimes blur strophic connections, it is equally common to treat strophes as "variations" individuated by thematic ideas or style of performance. Such treatment is akin to European theme and variation practice, in which the complexity of the diminutions often increases throughout the movement, while the strophes themselves are distinctly separated from one another by cadence and mode of variation procedure.

The problem remains, then, how to conceptualize the separated, distinct strophes as a single piece or movement, when a single overarching

Ex. 2-14a: Autumn Leaves

Ex. 2-14b: Autumn Leaves - Alternate

background presents an entirely alternate conception of the piece as a unique statement of harmonic closure in the large with small-scale hierarchical ramifications. In one sense, the problem could be resolved by viewing the cadence of the final variation as "more final" in its structural dominant-to-tonic close of the background; previous cadences are simply "less final," with some sense of the primary tone, usually $\hat{3}$ or $\hat{5}$, prolonged into the continuing strophe.

This is convenient enough, but the issue is best understood as an intrinsic weakness of applying the European model of large-scale structure, with its sense of single harmonic closure, to a body of work whose form, by nature strongly sectional, cadences repeatedly and nonhierarchically. In jazz, as in European theme and variations, variety of ornamentation and intricacy unifies the composition rather than the single harmonic statement of initiation-development-closure, represented at the highest level by the background. Hence, in jazz the background as a concept is best applied, usually, to a single strophe or chorus, since this is the smallest complete harmonic form. Moreover, it recalls the structure of the original composition (song) most closely.[47]

As noted above, in multi-chorus improvisation the soloist may avoid cadencing interior strophes in order to imply continuation to the next, but this need not be the case. Nonetheless, regardless of how the soloist connects the strophes melodically, the overall form of the solo is *of necessity* a linear set of choruses that may resist the forced hierarchization of inclusion within a single overarching background. Indeed, hearing a background over several strophes is sometimes as unnatural as hearing one over different solos or through an entire arrangement. This is the essential weakness of applying ideas derived from a European conception of musical form to a repetitive, nonhierarchic repertory; the sense of ritual, the ad hoc layout of much jazz improvisation at the largest scale fits uncomfortably with the concise, single closure of the background. Since there is no need to enforce ideas derived from European practice where they do not illuminate the music, my solution in this study, as usual, is practical: if it makes good analytical sense to suggest that a background voice-leading structure be heard as extending over several choruses, it is done—but this happens rarely. The background, as presented in the original "one-chorus" song usually applies most appropriately to one chorus of a solo.

Thus, multi-chorus improvisation, like its counterpart in classical variations, requires a more individual approach—the effect created by such a solo really might be more multiform than homogeneous, in which case voice-leading issues might apply more appropriately to each chorus taken as a single entity.[48] Most often, however, this issue simply will not arise here because most of the complete analyses to follow are in fact of one-chorus solos. (Longer solos are usually cited more generally or for specific short excerpts to make points where larger-scale analysis is unnecessary.) Further, Parker, restricted by the three-minute recording limit, rarely exceeded two choruses in the studio, where most of his best-known solos were recorded. In the single-chorus statement of a song-form, higher-level voice-leading reductions fulfill their function ideally and may be structurally informative, especially as they relate to the original melody.

Types of Thematic Patterns

The following are examples of *thematic patterns,* i.e., features of melodies,[49] whether composed or improvised. Though individuated below, these methods of pattern formation can also be interrelated or overlap. The first two types, arising through prolongation, are usually associated with voice-leading analyses:

(1) <u>Neighbor prolongation.</u> Here particular pitches may be featured and prolonged through neighboring at various levels. Tonic-triad pitches are most apt to receive such prolongations. As shown above, "Shaw 'Nuff" features nested neighbor patterns.

(2) <u>Scalar prolongational path.</u> These scalar paths, when sufficiently large-scale, can organize an entire melody and thereby achieve background status. The original melody of "Just Friends," (discussed in Ch. 4) is constructed through a pair of scalar paths (one partially implied). "All the Things You Are"[50] and "Autumn Leaves" (analyzed in the previous section) are constructed by means of scalar paths.

Between-level duplications and variations of prolongations are notably effective organizing devices, i. e. *diminutions.* In addition to these characteristic structural techniques, long familiar from Schenker's original work, other thematic patterns that typically figure in melodic organization include:

(3) <u>Emphasized single pitch</u>. These can also be prolonged, typically by neighbor motion (thematic pattern #1). Single pitches are often

emphasized through registral prominence, simple repetition, or some strikingly unusual treatment contextually. In registral prominence, a pitch is emphasized when it occurs outside the register of its surrounding pitches. An example of a pitch receiving unusual treatment is the cadence to D, the second degree of the scale, in the melody to "Cool Blues." (See Ch. 5, Ex. 5–2.)

(4) Sequence. These will sometimes generate larger-scale voice-leading lines and hence can be linked to thematic pattern #2. Familiar examples include "All the Things You Are" and "Autumn Leaves."

(5) Characteristic interval. Again, such intervals may be prolonged, giving rise to thematic patterns #1 or #2. "Embraceable You" (discussed in Ch. 4) has a characteristic interval of a third, given in its first three notes. The interval of a third is developed through the course of the melody.

(6) Open and Closed Space. That is, strategies of contrasting larger intervals, which open space, with stepwise motion that, in many instances, can be seen as filling it or providing some other means of closure. "Over the Rainbow"[51] opens with an ascending octave which is filled in through the gradual descent of the melody's A section. The "Palestrina curve," especially prevalent in the Renaissance, but influential in much tonal melody throughout history, is another such instance of spatial strategy.[52]

(7) Characteristic rhythm. Rhythms may be combined with or overlap pitch patterns to create motives (#8). Rhythms of pitches can be cited as thematic patterns at any structural level, but are most often associated with the note-to-note foreground in the creation of motives.[53]

(8) Motive. The familiar unit of thematic relationship. Motives are normally thought of as short sets of pitches—say two to eight—with a characteristic rhythm. Most melodies are constructed motivically. Motives can be "higher-level" (see #1 and #2), in which case they are less determinately characteristic of the piece at hand. Rhythm may be a less significant factor in the delineation of a higher-level motive.

Thus, voice-leading analysis charts the linear progress of a solo as it relates to harmonic function. To that extent, the voice-leading sketch, while partially "athematic" in its higher levels, relegates melodic function to a lesser position in order to clarify the harmonic. But insofar as harmonic progress can itself be thematic, or there may be thematic qualities independent of foreground rhythm, voice-leading analysis can be a useful tool for discovering them, as in thematic patterns #1 and #2 above. The other thematic patterns, #3-#8, are uncovered normally without the need of an intermediate voice-leading sketch, though hierarchies of relationship may exist there as well, especially in the area of rhythm.

Thematic Pattern, Motive and Formula in Improvisation

It is well-known that jazz improvisers repeat foreground melodic ideas from solo to solo. The foremost analysis of this aspect of the improviser's art has been Owens's study of Parker, but it has been discussed by others as well.[54] The duplication of melodic ideas from solo to solo places a difficult burden on the claim that jazz improvisation may be thematic while at the same time the soloist is apparently repeating material heard extensively elsewhere.

In addressing this issue, it is helpful to begin with a distinction among types of improvisation, as itemized by Kernfeld[55] from previous work by Hodeir[56] in jazz analysis:

(1) The paraphrase improvisation. Here the solo is clearly an embellishment of the original melody. This is conceptually the least problematic.
(2) The chorus phrase improvisation. The solo in this instance follows the form and harmony of the original melody, but is not based on its motives.
(3) Motivic improvisation. The solo is fashioned from motivic referents heard in the original melody.
(4) Formulaic improvisation. The solo repeats melodic ideas heard in other improvisations. Persistently recurring ideas are called "formulas."

As will emerge in the discussion to follow, this list is problematic. I shall suggest another way of organizing solos in bop style according to type.

There are two points of view from which we can begin to approach the issue of thematic relatedness: (1) What is the soloist trying to do thematically in the improvisation? (2) What sorts of thematic relatedness are we, as listeners, perceiving in the solo? In other words, the issue of thematic relatedness must be examined from the perspective of either the player or listener—either as intentionally projected by the artist or inferred by the analyst.

Let us begin with the types of improvisation, defined above as neutrally as possible, from the point of view of the soloist:

In paraphrase improvisation, it is clear that the player intends to interpret the melody in such a way that the listener recognizes it without difficulty. Since the intention of the player, in this case, is so unproblematic—even obvious—it might be concluded that the player's intention in the remaining types of improvisation can be similarly discerned.

But in other types of improvisation, the player's intention is far less evident. The least problematic of the three is motivic improvisation. Here, the soloist can be said to project motivic relatedness to the original melody, whenever foreground ideas are duplicated or developed in a methodical fashion. In these instances, it is often obvious that the soloist intends to base the improvisation on motives of the original melody.

But what about motivic relatedness that is more obscure or even borderline? Such relatedness could be coincidental. How can a listener know when the player intends the connection? A closely related problem arises when the soloist seems to be referring to the original melody through some melodic idea, but then applies the same idea—as a "formula"—to other solos on different melodies. For example, in the original melody of "Shaw 'Nuff" examined above (Ex. 2–9), a D-E♭-D neighbor motion was identified as a high-level motive that recurs in the bridge of Parker's improvisation (Ex. 2–10). However, the same arpeggiation pattern heard in the bridge of "Shaw 'Nuff" is found in the bridge of other Parker solos—"Red Cross," for example (see Ch. 3, Ex. 3–2)—where the resulting neighbor motion is not thematic.[57] Can we legitimately conclude that Parker, in "Shaw 'Nuff," was actually *developing* the original material? Such language implies intention; and from our point of view as listeners, it would seem that development was not intended. That is, although the relationship as it exists is reasonably convincing, it seems highly probable that Parker was not conscious of it.

Yet, many such relationships exist and may be discerned by a discriminating listener: thematic connections between solos and heads of which the soloist was unaware. Does the soloist's lack of intention in some way diminish the musical importance of the connection for the astute listener? That is, if the soloist does not intend the connection, is the relationship merely a "coincidence," and therefore unimportant to the musical result?

In trying to answer this clearly, it is important to notice that the network of possible thematic connections in music is far beyond any individual's conscious awareness. This same point is as true of improvisers as it is of composers, who, with the luxury of editing and reworking their material, are not constrained by the necessity of creation in real time—and at fast tempos. Potential musical connections, even cogent ones, are numerous—theoretically even infinite—such plethora of musical relatedness cannot possibly be at the conscious grasp of any musician, however gifted.

Hence, much musical connection that is cogent, musically telling, even exciting, may occur without the knowledge of its creator—that is, without the player intending the connection. Is it reasonable to assume that because the connection is unintentional, it is unimportant to the musical result aesthetically? It seems much more fruitful to view musical connections as they are *perceived*—that is, to shift the point of view, the burden of the analysis, to the listener.

For what is important in music with respect to its structure is what can be heard and felt, not what was intended: specifically, the relationships themselves apart from any speculations on the player's intentions—they are all we as listeners have to go on. Do they inform our sense of the solo? Do they enrich our understanding and deepen the musical experience? For any attempt to discern the intention of musical relatedness (beyond the fairly obvious, such as paraphrase or foreground motivic duplications) degenerates into unverifiable speculation. How is it possible for us to know what Parker was intending to project in his solos? Even a contemporary musician, who might be questioned soon after playing, will probably be unable to reconstruct in detail the actual thought process of the specific improvisation as real-time creation.

Investigation of the player's intentions is of course warranted for pedagogical or historical purposes. For example, musicians who wish to improvise well naturally would like insight as to the thought processes of players they emulate.[58] And certainly most of us would like to know what highly regarded players were thinking or intending, for its own obvious interest. But attempting to discern the intention of the soloist *for the purposes of adjudicating the importance of musical relationship* beyond the obvious is a can of worms best avoided.[59]

If Parker (or any soloist) reworks a similar network of pitches from solo to solo, it would seem likely, at first glance, that the use of the formula is not *intended* to relate thematically to the melody at hand. But such an attempt to discern intention creates problems: for surely Parker may have decided to use just this formula at this point in the solo *because* it does relate to the original melody; more generally, although the soloist has used the formula before, it fits particularly well to the moment at hand, so the soloist plays the formula with the intention of providing a connection to the head. But again, because there is no way of knowing what the soloist was trying to do, guessing the intention of the soloist is more troublesome than enlightening.

Ultimately, much more positive results obtain when the music is examined free from the attempt to know the unknowable. *Just because a group of notes is a formula and occurs in others solos does not preclude that formula from being all or partly thematic.* This follows directly from the conclusions, alluded to above, that the intention of the artist does not determine the ultimate value and effect of the created artwork.

Thus, the thought processes of the player with respect to the issues of formula and motivic connection in improvisation are often impenetrable, except in the most obvious cases. For the most part, this study will assume the listener's viewpoint, while taking into account the use of formula by the player, where relevant.

Curiously, a precise definition of formula as a building block for solos is probably quite impossible — an issue provocatively discussed in the literature on oral-epic poetry (which will be examined briefly in Ch. 6). Owens, in his study of Parker, is beset by the difficulty of defining "formula" as his "motives" (better called "formulas" to distinguish them from motives as thematic relationships[60]) are often so brief as to lose a sense of shape and identity. Further, they overlap in ways that make it impossible to distinguish among them distinctly. But again, the difficulty is not Owens's fault entirely: it is implicit in the concept itself of a formula, which by its very nature can resist pinning down.

Gushee, in his study of Lester Young's "Shoe Shine Boy," assembles sets of formulas whose criteria are surprisingly ad hoc. For example, one group of related formulas, called α, is assembled from a ". . . basic form (D), E, D♯, D in whole notes, also describable as a playing around with the fifth and sixth scale degrees or with the fourth and little fingers of the right hand."[61] The α-formulas themselves vary widely in melodic content. Another set ζ of formulas consists of "blues clichés"[62] of, again, disparate melodic content (though all emphasize the blue third). Despite the wide variance and criteria for inclusion, Gushee's categorization of formulas is largely persuasive — which shows just how elusive the idea can be.

Despite the difficulty in pinning down a group of improvisational formulas, Kernfeld[63] shows that the concept is perhaps best described as a network of melodic possibilities with major and minor variants, which often include other formulas as constituent parts. It is usually quite difficult to specify the notes of a formula exactly. Nor do statistics of note frequency and repetition settle the matter in any definite way, since note-counting does not factor in the shape, distinctiveness, or contextual placement of the melodic idea in question.

Kernfeld's solution—the formula as a network of linked melodic ideas—is similar conceptually to Wittgenstein's "family portrait" model of overlapping relatedness. The formula may vary widely, but will usually retain significant enough features to be identified as "the" formula. With this caveat in mind, let us agree to accept the convenience of referring to a specific formula (say, from Owens's list), so long as we remain aware that the actual music might vary considerably from its given notation in the list. As a family of related formulas gradually transforms to some other, it becomes an analytical judgment when to change its name.

As noted above in the "Shaw 'Nuff" example, a formula used in one solo might be motivically related to the head, whereas in another performance, the same formula (with the understanding that "same" usually means "similar") might now be unrelated (in any significant sense). Serendipitous as the motivic connection might be, it should not be dismissed as irrelevant, since the accident of its relatedness does not undermine the fact of its relatedness.

Throughout Parker's improvisations, there are numerous and cogent instances of relatedness between his formulas and the motivic material in the head, as will be demonstrated in the analytical chapters to follow. Indeed, such "unexpectedly thematic" improvisation suggests that Hodier-Kernfeld's second, third, and fourth types of improvisation can sometimes be linked together: that while the soloist is repeating melodic formulas played in other solos (#4) during a chorus-phrase improvisation that avoids obvious reference to the original melody (#2), underlying thematic patterns may in fact provide that link in ways that may not be immediately obvious, producing a type of motivic improvisation— (#3). Hence, it might be conceptually more useful to distinguish *three* types of solos:

(1) Paraphrase improvisation: obvious relationship to the head in which the underlying melody is accounted for much of the time: more simply, embellishment.
(2) Thematic Improvisation: relationship to the head, which at some times may be clearly discernible, but at other times more abstruse.

(3) Harmonic improvisation: the melodic qualities of the head do not seem to affect the solo motivically.

As will become evident in the analyses, use of formula by the improviser is common to all three types of improvisation (though occurring less at slower tempos). Further speculation on the significance of the relationship between formula and motive will be reserved for the concluding chapter after a sampling of Parker improvisations has been examined for thematic connection to the original melody.

Chapter 3

Rhythm Changes

Rhythm Changes as a Formal Model

With 32-bar AABA form and harmonies based on the circle of fifths, rhythm changes has been a pervasive vehicle for jazz improvisation for more than 60 years. Its structure was analyzed in Example 2–1 in Ch. 2. Please refer to that example for the following more detailed comments on rhythm changes.

During the A section the tonic harmony is prolonged in two-bar units. In actual performance, the rhythm section will tend to articulate only the more important of these chords, usually including: (1) the tonic established at the beginning of the A section and repeated in m. A-5, (2) the change to the dominant at m. A-4, (3) the subdominant at m. A-6, and, finally, (4) the tonic or dominant concluding the A section. These skeletal chords can be seen in the reduction given in the second staff from the bottom staff of the A-section system in Ex. 2–1. At the end of any given A section, the players either cadence to the tonic at m. A-8 for continuation to the bridge (B section), or proceed to another A section via a turnaround.[64]

The first chord of the bridge is D7, a chromatically modified harmony that initiates a chain of dominant sevenths returning to the tonic B♭ at the subsequent A section. This dominant-seventh pattern is derived from the A section by quadrupling the harmonic rhythm from two beats to eight, modifying the qualities of the chords, and backing up in the circle of fifths to the D7 chord. While the large-scale harmonic function of the bridge is to prolong the tonic of the A section, its immediate effect is to refresh the overall form with contrasting dominant-seventh chord qualities and varied harmonic rhythm.

The simplicity and elegance of rhythm changes account for its continuing popularity in jazz: since the two-, four-, and eight-bar subdivisions are easily internalized, the soloist is free to create complications that play off against the large-scale regularity of the form. That is, the simplicity and logic of the harmonic structure allow the soloist a great deal of melodic freedom. Further, substantial modifications to and substitutions of the basic harmonies are easily accommodated without any loss of coherence or identity.

Red Cross

Let us begin with an example of early Charlie Parker, his "Red Cross" recordings from 1944. In these performances Parker is a guest soloist with a swing-based ensemble, the Tiny Grimes Quintet.[65] These recordings are Parker's first professionally recorded rhythm-changes improvisations and are among Parker's first recordings as a featured soloist.[66] After examining the two takes of "Red Cross," we shall turn to "Shaw 'Nuff," a classic bop rhythm-changes performance, though recorded only eight months later.

Red Cross—Original Melody

The melody of "Red Cross," which appears in Ex. 3–1, must have been worked out in part at the studio, since its bridge is rewritten for the second take. The head is based on a single phrase that emphasizes Bb in both the Bb4 and Bb3 registers. The C5-Bb4 motive is labeled X, and the thematic octave Bb's labeled Y. Prolonged from m. A-1, the Bb4 proceeds briefly to Db5, the ninth of the bII six-nine chord in m. A-6, before returning to Bb4 for the cadence. Thus, a î-B3̂-î large-scale structure is projected overall, but is quite unusual insofar as the blue third is supported by a bII six-nine chord rather than by the more common dominant. In the solos to follow, the musicians avoid the progression to bII, found in the head, and substitute standard rhythm changes.

The bridge of take 1 is rather awkward melodically. For example, the D5 in m. B-1 proceeds too quickly to C5 in m. B-3, an 11th not comfortably supported by the G7 harmony. This pitch is thereafter prolonged for the duration of the bridge until rejoining C5 for the A3 section. Similarly, the A4 of m. B-3 does not connect convincingly to any later pitches of the bridge.

The improved bridge of take 2 is both easier to play and melodically more compelling, since its various voice-leading lines converge effectively to the A3 section. The C5, awkward in the first take as an 11th of G7, is resolved directly to B4. Further, the lines consisting of D5 (m. B-1), C5 (m. B-3), and B4 (m. B-3); then C5 (m. B-5), Bb4 (m. B-7), A4

Ex. 3-1: Red Cross

(m. B-7) lead effortlessly to the A3 section. Parker does, however, alter the sequence in m. B-8 to emphasize the connection to C5 (motive X) at the start of section A3.

To sum up, the principal motivic thrust of "Red Cross" is a prolonged Bb3-Bb4, motive Y, with motive X as C5-Bb4 at the foreground. The large-scale movement to Db5 in m. A-6 proceeds through C5 to the cadence on Bb4.

Ex. 3-2: Red Cross - Takes 1 and 2

Red Cross—Take 1

The two takes of Parker's "Red Cross" solo are superimposed on Ex. 3–2. Let us begin with a discussion of take 1. Emphasis on the pitch B♭, the main idea of the original melody, is established in Parker's first phrase: both B♭4 and B♭3 are clearly articulated as motive Y. A skip to B♭4 in m. A1-6 emphasizes this pitch further as motive X appears and begins a phrase that closes the A1 section—also on motive X—in m. A1-7.

The A2 section begins with a familiar Parker arpeggiation figure—yet Parker's choice of this formula thematically highlights a B♭4 at m. A2-4[67] as motive X′: C-B♭ filled in by C♭. Perhaps because this arpeggiation pattern anticipates the texture of the bridge too literally, Parker avoids it in the second take. The A2 section ends with a virtual quotation from the original melody, including quarter notes C4 and B♭3 as motive X. This

rather maladroit foreground referent is also omitted in take 2. However at this same place, in both takes, Parker makes another explicit connection to the original melody through the neighboring C4's and D♭4's.[68]

Parker begins the bridge with an arpeggiation pattern[69] that will be repeated in "Shaw 'Nuff," the next example in this chapter. Yet again B♭4 is emphasized—this time on the third beats of mm. B-2 and B-3. The sixteenth-note passage beginning in m. B-5 is also completed to B♭4 at

Ex. 3-2: Red Cross - Takes 1/2

m. B-6 and includes two appearances of motive X. The second appearance of X (m. B-7) features Parker outlining a superimposed E♭ triad over the F7 harmony. That this is the prolonged harmony (rather than the simpler F7 chord with the tensions resolved) is shown by the voice leading in m. B-8, where the G4 proceeds to G♭4, then to F4 in m. A3-1. (This basic voice leading is repeated in take 2.) The C5 at the close of m. B-6 eventually cadences to B♭4 in section A3. The phrase leading from the bridge to the A3 section features much B♭3.

Section A3 of the solo closes with prominent iterations of B♭4 and motive X'. Indeed, B♭4 is heard in each bar from m. A3-3 to the end of the solo.

Parker's first take is centered around the original melody's structural projection of B♭. Yet there is little feeling of motion and evolution in the solo, possibly because of its too-explicit motivic evocation of the original melody. Since Parker never achieves clear movement away from B♭4, the take never articulates a convincing large-scale structural framework.[70]

Red Cross—Take 2

Take 2, though more ambiguous in projecting the octave B♭'s, is still convincing in asserting thematic features of the original melody. Parker establishes a darker mood at once with a blues-like phrase featuring both ♭5 and ♭3. This phrase connects to the original melody by beginning and ending on the thematic pitch, B♭3. The second phrase, at m. A1-4, begins with the equally thematic B♭4 accented by pick-up sixteenths as motive X'. The B♭4 is re-articulated in m. A1-6, before the section closes on B♭3. Parker's modification of m. A1-5 in the second take—its strong articulation of the G4 and the syncopated pause on E♭4—anticipates and accents the harmonic motion to E♭ major, and thus prepares the resolution to D4 and B♭ major in m. A1-6.

The A2 section continues the blues-like quality of the solo's opening, but moves into the higher register.[71] Introduced by a triplet at the end of section A1, the D5 and D♭5 jointly form a blue primary tone, labeled B3̂, which establishes a sense of large-scale structure missing in take 1. The pitch B♭4, prolonged through section A1, functions very much like a Schenkerian *Anstieg*, a preparation of the primary tone, which helps create a sense of large-scale progression from the first to the second A section.

The D5-D♭5 in m. A2-1 begin a voice-leading line, dexterously completed by the sixteenths of mm. A2-3,4. In this run, the thematic C5 and B♭4 as motive X are highlighted: that is, they are not only peaks in the figure, but are also skipped to. The end of the A2 section recalls the corresponding passage from take 1, but the effect of the direct quotation is softened.

The bridge in take 2 is smoother than in take 1, largely because the four-bar phrase of the first half is balanced symmetrically by the single phrase of the second half.[72] The voice leading of take 2, however, repeats the motions first heard in take 1. Motive X in m. B-7 is replaced by the subtler X'.

The first half of the A3 section recalls take 2's opening. Parker cadences the upper, structural register emphatically in m. A3-7. Thus, take 2 articulates a clear higher-level architecture and, with its blues-like feel, effectively contrasts the head's rather static emphasis of Bb3 and Bb4.

Both of Parker's solos on "Red Cross" mirror the large-scale structural features of the original melody, yet the second take is superior in that, among other things, it mirrors them more indirectly. An important point about the nature of thematic reference is that its existence does not guarantee superior results: direct references to the head can sometimes be *too* specific or heavy-handed, thereby overbalancing a need for adequate variety in the solo. In the "Red Cross" solos, the second take is superior in its greater subtlety and its articulation of a convincing high-level voice-leading progression. In retrospect, take 1 comes across as a kind of warm-up—an opportunity for Parker to marshal his concentration, accustom himself to the head, and adjust to the ambience of recording with the Grimes ensemble in the studio.

Shaw 'Nuff

For comparison to "Red Cross," let us now turn to "Shaw 'Nuff,"[73] which, though early bop, is mature Parker. A typically fine Bb rhythm-changes performance, it reveals the structural depth of Parker's best work. Many of the foreground ideas heard in "Red Cross" reappear in "Shaw 'Nuff," but the overall motivic emphasis changes.

Shaw 'Nuff—Original Melody

Example 3–3 is a transcription and analysis of the original melody of "Shaw 'Nuff." Its first two pitches, D5 and F5, define the tune's principal motive, labeled M. The repeat of D5-F5 in m. A1-1 with D5 now *on* the beat reveals a simple, but fundamental idea of swing in bop lines: displacing a pattern relative to the meter. The A4-C5 third in m. A1-2 echoes motive M, further establishing the figure. Motive M reappears between mm. A1-7,8 and is composed out there at two larger-scale levels. It is also modified to a D5-F4 sixth (labeled M') and appears twice in m. A1-3. The F5-A4 sixth in m. A1-1 is labeled M": the first three pitches of the head are transposed two bars later to produce M'.

Throughout the A1 section the D5 undergoes a variety of neighbor prolongations, labeled N, at the middleground. Of the several shown on

Ex. 3-3: Shaw 'Nuff (Melody)

the analysis, the most important is the large-scale neighbor E♭5 at m. A1-6. This pitch, at a slightly lesser structural level, also functions in passing connection to F5: motive M composed out.

In the second A section, the melody is altered at m. A2-7 to present motive M composed out as an ascending figure. Measure A2-8, rather than cadencing to the tonic B♭4, provides a link to the bridge via diminutions of the D5-E♭5 neighbor idea.

Ex. 3-3: Shaw 'Nuff (Melody)

The bridge continues the idea of long-term neighboring. The most important are the motions from Db5 (C#5) in m. B-3 to D5 in m. B-4 and F#5 in m. B-5 to F5 in m. B-7. The latter pitch resolves the F#5 in m. B-5 and also arises thematically from the D5 in m. B-4, thus providing a climax to the melody. It is followed by D5, as motive M, to create the pickup to section A3. The importance of the climactic F5 is further intensified through its small-scale neighboring by the G5 triplet.

Section A3 repeats the A2 material, but with appropriate modifications so that motive M, composed-out in m. A3-7, finally cadences to B♭4. Given the cadence here to B♭4, it is possible to posit a large-scale voice-leading structure for the piece as whole. Although F5 is accented on the first beat of the m. A1-1, and is strongly rearticulated at the end of the bridge, it is the D5, finally, that seems to be more specifically prolonged by the neighbor motions throughout the piece. Yet, rather than make this choice, it might be better to note that ambiguity of primary tone is essential to the piece's structure; hence, the tonic F5-D5-B♭4 triad is *itself* composed out in the large, with a final cadence to B♭4 postponed until the end of the tune.

Thus the original melody of "Shaw 'Nuff" is characterized by thematic emphasis on the D5-F5 third as motive M, the F4-D5 sixth as M′, and neighboring motions of M, especially D5. Motive M eventually resolves to B♭4 in m. A3-8. The analytic sketch also points out additional neighbor motives in the foreground and the prevalence of composed-out thirds.

Shaw 'Nuff—Improvisation

The transcription and analysis of Parker's "Shaw 'Nuff" solo appear in Ex. 3-4. Parker's opening phrase establishes the 3̂ of the basic structure and composes out the thematic M′ sixth, F4-D5. Motive M′ is then recapitulated in the last two beats of m. A1-7 and the first beat of m. A1-8. Thus from the outset the F4-D5 sixth appears as a major motivic force in the solo—it frames the A1 section, as a dyad and in composed-out form.

Throughout the A1 section motive M as D4-F4 is prolonged at the middleground—it is neighbored by G4-E♭4 at mm. A1-5,6. This neighboring parallels the D5-E♭5-D5 neighbor motions of the original melody.

The A2 section begins with a quotation from the head (from m. A1-5), as noted in the example. The pitch D5 is elaborated through neighbor motion to E♭5 in mm. A2-1,2. Afterwards, the D4-F4 third is prolonged again through the neighbor motion to E♭4-G4, as in section A1.

As pointed out in Ch. 2, the bridge features an extended prolongation of the background D5 by E♭5, which, though dissonant, is itself prolonged through the first four bars. At the conclusion of the bridge in mm. B-7,8, the D5 is joined thematically to F5—a climactic appearance

Ex. 3-4: Shaw 'Nuff - Solo

of motive M in the original register of the head. The original melody features a similar climactic appearance of M at this point. The reference is further reinforced by M″, the A4-F5 sixth.

The pitch E♭5 in the bridge neighbors the primary tone, D5, while in the lower register, the D4-F4 third prolonged from the A1 and A2 sections creates voice-leading lines that culminate in its neighbor, E♭4-G4, by m. B-7. This lower third resolves thematically to D4-F4 at m. A3-2.

Ex. 3-4: Shaw 'Nuff (Solo)

At the beginning of section A3, Parker quotes the head again, as noted on the sketch: that is, the first six beats merge the first and fifth bars of the head's A3 section. In the lower register, motive M enters at m. A3-2, thematically neighbored by E♭4-G4. The structural cadence to 1̂ (B♭4) over the Edim7th anticipates the harmonic resolution of the chord changes at m. A3-8. Parker's last melodic phrase ushers in Gillespie's solo.

The liquidation in section A3 is largely created by chromatic lines and the breakdown of Parker's implied polyphony. The D4-F4 third figures all the more prominently in mm. A3-2,3, therefore, since there are few other events prolonged at all. The cadential B♭4-D♭5 third together with Parker's sliding intonations in mm. A1-1,2, and m. A2-2, account for the subtle undercurrent of blues felt throughout the solo.

Parker elaborates the structural idea of "Shaw 'Nuff" by highlighting and composing out motive M—often through neighbor motions. The F4-D5 sixth (motive M') also appears thematically throughout the solo. Parker's final A section compactly sums up the basic structural elements of both the head and the improvisation.

Example 3–5 superimposes the middleground voice leading and motives of "Red Cross" and "Shaw 'Nuff" in order to summarize the overall differences between the solos. Duplications of foreground motives, particularly in the bridges, do not detract from their thematic individuality. An important point that should be clear from the example is that any thematic differences between "Red Cross" and "Shaw 'Nuff" do not result from subtle harmonic differences between the heads.[74] That is, relatively small differences between the comping of the rhythm sections or the heads' original changes cannot be cited as motivating the dramatic structural differences between the solos, which, instead, derive from thematic association with the the original melodies. Neither does the presence of overlapping B♭ rhythm-changes formulas detract at all from Parker's solos referring distinctly to their original melodies.

Shaw 'Nuff—Other Improvisational Features

The preceding section emphasized thematic connections between the original melody of "Shaw 'Nuff" and Parker's improvisation to show how this solo was distinguished from the "Red Cross" solos; further analysis of "Shaw 'Nuff" is given in this section to elucidate fine points of Parker's style and bop style as a whole. Moreover, Owens's formulas will be examined in greater detail in order to clarify how Parker uses them to create thematic reference.

Parker's phrasing and accents account for much of the solo's drive. For example, the opening phrase articulates a B♭4-D5 third, which initiates voice-leading lines that proceed downward, via A4-C5 and A♭4-C♭4, to G4-B♭4 in m. A1-4. Parker in fact is using a melodic formula here, Owens's M. 9, which occurs in both sections A1 and A2.[75] But Parker's choosing to include it here does in fact create a thematic connection to the head: the C5-C♭5-B♭4 occurs in the first bar of the original melody.

Ex. 3-5: Red Cross - Shaw 'Nuff Middlegrounds

The B♭4 in m. A1-2, which initiates a descending voice-leading line, is accented off the beat (on the "and" of one), and precedes a comparatively long space. When the melody picks up again in m. A1-3, C5 and C♭5 are accented, but *on* the beat (beats three and four), and create the expectation of another accented B♭4 on the downbeat of m. A1-4. Yet, by choosing to play formula M. 9 here, Parker delays the B♭4 until the second beat of m. A1-4 and fills the space created on the downbeat with the thematic F4-D4 third.

The opening F4 combines thematically with D4 in m. A1-3 to create another pair of voice-leading lines linked by thirds. The two lines in double thirds intersect at the G4 prolonged in mm. A1-5,6. The lower-register activity in mm. A1-6,7 creates still other lines which, with the return of the upper register in mm. A1-7,8, brings about a separation of voices again. Thus, the A1 section features a voice-leading wedge, first compressing at m. A1-6, then widening abruptly at the section's end.

The lower-register passage from m. A1-5 to m. A1-7, first two beats, is a composite of motivic formulas[76]—indeed, the passage is almost duplicated in section A2. Yet this conjunction of formulas creates the D4-F4 to E♭4-G4 neighboring that thematically reflects the original melody. Further, when Parker departs from the formulas on the third beat of m. A1-7, it is to return to the critically thematic F4-D5 sixth.

After the high G5 beginning section A2 and eclipsing the solo's range thus far, Parker returns to the earlier melodic formula (M. 9) for a recomposition of the thematic descent from D5 to F4. Measures A2-3,4 vary the accents of the corresponding bars in section A1: the pitches C5, B4, and B♭4, again part of the motivic formula, are shifted back two beats; the thematic F4-D4 is again interpolated between C♭4 and B♭4. Measures A2-6,7 closely recall mm. A1-6,7, but in the seventh and eight bars Parker cadences in the lower register with D4-B♭3 rather than return to F4-D5 as in the first A section. In broadest terms, section A2 recomposes section A1—it begins higher, works through similar material, then closes in the lower register.

Sections A1 and A2 are phrased similarly: the first two bars are separated from the remainder of the section, and each section ends with a relatively long silence. Parker reverses the A-section phrasing in the bridge, which begins with a long phrase of five and a half bars, while the last two bars are treated separately. Measures B-7,8 begin a phrase extending into section A3, the only time a sectional division is overlapped. This last section contrasts the first part of the solo by featuring short, choppy phrases, which strengthen the section's function as concluding the solo and also serve to isolate the cadential phrase in m. A3-6.

Measures B-1 to B-7 contrast the melodic descents of the A sections with relatively static arpeggios.[77] For example, the lower notes cluster around D4 (including E4, E♭4, D4, and B3 as chord tones) while the upper tones cling to D5 (including E♭5, C5, and B♭4). At the same time, these bars disclose a descending thirds line amidst the arpeggios: A4-C5 in m. B-1 proceeds to E4-G4 (m. B-5) and eventually to E♭4-G4 (m. B-7). This third, heard as a neighbor in sections A1 and A2, finally proceeds to D4-F4 in section A3. Thus, Parker at m. B-1 breaks away texturally and motivically from his A-section material, but reasserts D4-F4 as section A3 begins.

The accents of the bridge are both satisfying and unexpected. In m. B-1, the E♭5 is stressed on the third beat. In m. B-2 the C5 is accented on the "and" of the second beat, but in m. B-3 the accent returns to the third beat. The third-beat accent is reinforced in m. B-4, but Parker then thwarts this pattern in m. B-5 by accenting two pitches unexpectedly—on the "and" of two and on four. Finally, the downbeat of m. B-6 is accented, a beat not emphasized thus far. For the pitches climaxing the end of the bridge, including motive M, the accents return to the off-beat: the "and" of four in m. B-7, the "and" of one in m. B-8, and the "and" of three in m. B-8.

Neighbor motion, so characteristic of the A sections and the original melody, is important in the bridge as well and takes place between entire chords. So, for example, the third and fourth beats of the first three bars of the bridge provide neighbor motions at the level of the changes.

The A3 section, in contrast, features fewer accents and use of melodic formulas. Parker here is winding the solo down and, in effect, seems to allude to its main structural features more casually (despite the quotation in m. A3-1) than in the main exposition of the solo in sections A1 and A2. Nevertheless, it can be argued that whenever formulas appear in this solo, there is some thematic reason for their use: the underlying structure of the tune pervades the solo.

Thriving on a Riff

"Thriving on a Riff"[78] was recorded six months later than "Shaw 'Nuff"—roughly the same amount of time separating "Shaw 'Nuff" from "Red Cross." Still a relatively early recording for Parker, "Thriving on a Riff" projects his growing self-confidence with well-knit, two-chorus solos in each of the takes.[79]

Thriving on a Riff—Original Melody

The original melody's pervasive use of thirds produces cramped phrases spanning limited ranges (Ex. 3–6). Arpeggiated and composed-out thirds are contrasted throughout. For example, the first two pitches of the melody, Bb3 and D4, are immediately filled in by the same pitches composed out in contrary motion; similarly, the opening bar ascends through a D4-Eb4-F4

Ex. 3-6: Thriving on a Riff (Melody)

third, which then appears dyadically on the fourth beat. This D4 to F4 rise within m. A-1 is contrasted by a longer descent through m. A-3.

Although thirds abound throughout the piece, the D4-F4 third serves through prolongation as the melody's principal motivic element. The A section is unified in the large by the various passing motions between the D4 and F4. The first ending closes on the D4-F4 interval, the second ending closes ambiguously on C4, and the third ending rounds off the piece with a cadence through C4 to B♭3. Hence the D4-F4 third unifies the piece as a whole.

In the bridge, the D4-F4 third is modified to D4-F♯4 at m. B-2, D4-F4 at m. B-3, E4-G4 at m. B-5, and E♭4-G4 at m. B-7 before returning at section A3. The interval is stated for the last time at m. A3-7, beat 2, and is composed out in that bar as well.

Movement from D4 to B♭3 at the melody's close completes the large-scale projection of the B♭ triad. Other prominent D4-F4 thirds can be found spanning m. A-5 to m. A-7 (composed out), joining m. A1-6 to m. A1-7, in m. A1-8, in m. A2-7 (and m. A3-7), and in m. B-3 (composed out).[80]

Thriving on a Riff—Take 1

Parker's solos on "Thriving on a Riff" (Ex. 3–7) relate convincingly to the original melody. Not only is the character of the improvisations similar to the head,[81] but the D4-F4 third also assumes major motivic prominence throughout, both as a dyad and in composed-out form. The more general use of thirds found in the original melody pervades Parker's solo as well.

Take 1 features the same large-scale structure to be heard in take 3, but perhaps worked out in a slightly less successful manner. The articulation of D4-F4 is evident throughout this first take. The first phrase sets up D4-F4 as accented quarter notes at m. 1A1-3, while the 1A1 section ends with D4-F4 and recalls the solo's opening phrase. In fact, these are common formulas: m. 1A1-3 is Owens's M. 12B; m. 1A1-7 is M. 6A. Parker's choice of formulas is once again influenced by the character and structural properties of the original tune.

Parker begins the 1A2 section by establishing the higher register with a prolonged D5. The D4-F4 third soon returns, however, now composed out from m. 1A2-6 to m. 1A2-7.

The melody of the first bridge extends the D7 harmony to sharp eleven (G♯) and thirteen (B). This G♯4-B4 third can be followed downwards through the voice leading of the bridge until its culmination on D4-F4 at section 1A3: D4 at m. 1A3-1 leading to F4 at m. 1A3-2. The 1A3 section

Ex. 3-7: Thriving on a Riff - Takes 1/3

recapitulates material from the 1A1 section—including the quarter-note D4-F4 phrase at m. 1A3-4 and the D4-F4 at m. 1A3-7.

The second chorus begins with Parker's familiar "High Society" phrase[82]—but this figure in fact ends thematically on F4 and D4 at m. 2A1-3. Given so much emphasis on D4-F4 thus far in the solo, Parker may have felt compelled to return to composing out the higher register at the start of the 2A2 section. Yet even here the standard Parker figure[83] beginning in m. 2A2-3 is ultimately extended to a composed-out D4-F4 at the section's conclusion.

Parker adroitly turns to sixteenth notes at m. 2B2-1. But their inclusion continues to be thematic: each of the runs begins on D4, with the pick-ups leading first to F#4, then to F4.[84] In m. 2B-5, E4 continues a

Ex 3-7· Thriving on a Riff - Takes 1/3

voice-leading progression through to E♭4—featured in mm. 2B-7,8—finally culminating in the D4-F4 motive at m. 2A3-1. The principal motive is composed out through the final section with the resolution to B♭3
delayed until the very end.

Thriving on a Riff—Take 3

At once, Parker establishes both the A and B sections of the original
melody: not only is D4-F4 present dyadically and in composed-out form,

Ex. 3-7: Thriving on a Riff - Takes 1/3

but the entire first bar of the solo is also a transposition of the melody's m. B-1, offset by a beat. Within this bar, the D4-F4 third is first composed out chromatically, then diatonically, then stated dyadically. The same interval returns to complete the 1A1 section in m. 1A1-7. Hence, section 1A1 is framed by *F4-D4*-C4-B♭3-A3-C4 at the top and C4-B♭3-A3-B♭3-*D4-F4* in m. 1A1-7. Further, m. 1A1-2 recalls m. A2-8 of the original melody and its sense of incompleteness on C4.

Ex. 3-7: Thriving on a Riff - Takes 1/3

Section 1A2 begins with F5-D5, i.e., the motive transposed up an octave. It is then composed out from m. 1A2-3 to m. 1A2-4, before the line
returns to the lower register of F4-D4, stated in m. 1A2-5 and used to conclude the section. Hence, Parker in the 1A2 section establishes the F-D motivic pattern in the higher register while continuing to refer to it in the lower.

The first bridge extends the chromaticisms of the original melody
much as in take 1: the original melody's F#4-A4 is replaced by G#4-B4,

the sharp eleventh and thirteenth of D7. This third then proceeds through F#4-A4 to F4-A4 (m. 1B-3) and E4-G4 (mm. 1B-5,6). But rather than returning casually to D4-F4 at section 1A3, Parker inserts an angular build-up to the sharp-nine A♭ in m. 1B-8 to reinforce D5-F5 in the higher register. The tension created at the start of section 1A3 is soon dissipated by the D4-B♭3 cadence in m. 1A3-7.

References to F-D abound in Parker's second chorus as well. The 2A1 section begins by articulating F5-D5 with chromatic embellishments. The 2A2 section recalls mm. 1A1-1,2 before sixteenth-note flourishes settle on F4. The section then concludes somewhat enigmatically on D4. The bridge, section 2B, is simpler by way of contrast—the F#4-A4 moving down in straightforward fashion, almost duplicating the voice leading of the original melody's bridge. The F4 in m. 2B-7 anticipates the F4 of 2A3.

The final section of the solo begins by connecting F4 and D5 through triplet scales as a parting reference to the higher register. The chorus then concludes with an emphatic repetition of D4-F4 in m. A3-8. The closure to B♭3 recalls the original melody's cadence.

The take 3 improvisation as a whole features a prolonged D4-F4 third with smaller-scale closures to B♭3 occurring throughout—in particular D4-B♭3 at the end of the first chorus.[85] Section 2A3 cadences the upper register in m. 2A3-1 to m. 2A3-5. Finally D4 enters in m. 2A3-7 (the first D4 in section 2A3) to set up the lower-register cadence through C4 to a delayed B♭3 at the start of the next chorus. The delay serves to emphasize further the final statements of the D4-F4 motive in m. 2A3-8.

Parker establishes the primacy of the D4-F4 motive, the basis of the original melody, in each of his takes. Further, Parker retains the general character of the theme, tailoring his phrases so as to recapture the knotty mood of the original. Take 1 is a fine effort, but is eclipsed by take 3 in both internal subtlety and external relationship to the original material.

Crazeology

The defining feature of "Crazeology"[86] is a modification of the rhythm-changes chordal structure with a II-V-I in G♭, or ♭VI,[87] in the fifth and six bars, as shown in Ex. 3-8a. The background sketch in Ex. 3-8b shows that the large-scale structure of the head incorporates the b$\hat{2}$ (C♭) into a basic $\hat{3}$-$\hat{2}$-$\hat{1}$ plan. The resulting $\hat{3}$-$\hat{2}$, b$\hat{2}$-$\hat{1}$ phrasing of the fundamental line is in fact the basic motive of the original melody at the large-scale: Q (see Ex. 3–8c),which appears in diatonic forms in the A section and chromatic forms (Q') in the bridge.

Ex. 3-8a: Crazeology Head

Ex. 3-8b: Crazeology Background (A Section)

Ex. 3-8c: Crazeology Thematic Structure

The background sketch of this well-constructed tune (Ex. 3–8b) also shows descending scales, first in B♭ major, then in G♭ major . From them we can glimpse the motivation behind Parker's opening idea on take D (Ex. 3–8d) which appears nowhere else in the session and which helps to elevate it over the other solos in effectiveness: the rapidly ascending B♭ (Lydian) scales. With them, the middleground descending B♭ scale of the head, modified with an E natural, appears at the opening of Parker's solo in diminution and inverted.

In m. A1-3 of take D Parker begins a familiar formula (Owens's M. 9), heard in previous B♭ rhythm-changes solos: yet here, he interrupts the formula with a leap to D5 in m. A1-4. This interruption establishes the D5 as an important pitch of the solo and emphasizes its connection to D♭5 in m. A1-5.

Beginning in m. A1-5, at the temporary tonal shift to G♭ via II-V-I, Parker's line closely approximates the overall motion of the head at this same point. Further, both head and solo feature the important motion from D5 to D♭5. Parker creates thematic references throughout all four takes by reflecting this large-scale motion whenever it occurs. In take D, the emphasis is even more explicit: D♭5 is the pitch of significance in all three A sections at the shift to G♭; in Ex. 3–8d the interplay of these pitches is bracketed throughout. Parker then proceeds to resolve the D5 to B♭4 in m. A3-7, a resolution avoided in the earlier A sections of this take.

The large-scale motion from G5-F5 in the bridge of the head is duplicated in take D as well. Parker accents the G5 at the beginning of the bridge in order to emphasize its significance: its prominence insures the aural connection to F5 in m. B-5, atop the familiar formula (M. 5C), which thus serves a motivic function through indirect reference to the head.

Wee

As a contrast to the more thought-out and controlled studio sessions just discussed, let us glance briefly at a well-known live recording: "Wee"[88] as performed at the Massey Hall concert of 1953. Otherwise known as "Allen's Alley," "Wee" is a head based on rhythm changes in B♭ with an improvised bridge. The Massey Hall concert features an amazingly fast, sure, and well-recorded live performance in which Parker still manages to hint at the head in his solo, despite the more informal live venue.[89]

"Wee" is a simple, almost riff-like tune, based on a compound melody of descending scales, as shown in Ex. 3–9a. The accented 3̂, D5, at the tune's opening initiates an octave line to D4, as 3̂ in the lower register.

Ex. 3-8d: Crazeology - Take D

This main middleground motion is complemented by a descent from an implied B♭4 to B♭3. Through the interaction of these lines, the B♭4-D5 third can be seen as a motivating structure in the tune.

While this remarkable solo could be analyzed at length, for purposes of space only the beginning and ending of Parker's solo will be cited. The opening phrase of the solo (Ex. 3–9b) is especially evocative of the original melody, developing it virtually in diminution: the descending scale from 3̂, an emphasized B♭3-D4 third at the end of the descent, and a more arpeggiated rise to B♭4. (The 1A1 section also ends by echoing the lower B♭3-D4 third.) The concluding phrase of Parker's solo at the end of the 3A3 section effectively closes on the D-B♭ third in both upper and lower registers (Ex. 3–9c). The final notes Parker plays at the beginning of the next chorus are a lead-in for Gillespie).

Lester Leaps In

An extravagant, almost experimental live B♭ rhythm-changes performance can be sampled on a recording at the Rockland Palace, New York City.[90] Like "Wee," the uptempo performance of "Lester Leaps In" is one of the more thrilling live Parker solos available. It contains virtually all of the major Parker rhythm-changes formulas, linked together more for virtuoso, spontaneous display than careful, thought-out composition. In such a venue, more informal than even the Massey Hall concert, connections to the original melody are far less likely to occur; the soloist is, appropriately, responding more to the excitement of the occasion. Nevertheless, Parker manages to work effectively with the structure of the head, if more loosely than in "Wee," and certainly more informally than in any of the studio sessions.

The head of "Lester Leaps In" is based on a simple riff of the tonic triad, with special emphasis on the tonic pitch. While there is not much evidence of melodic reference to the head in the first part of the solo, about halfway through Parker returns to the riff and treats it in sequence with a transposition to E♭. Further, throughout the performance, the band echoes and reinforces the accents of the riff, as if to let Parker play *around* its metrical structure, highlighting it through rhythmic and contrapuntal interplay. After treating the riff in sequence, Parker keeps its presence alive by centering much of the remainder of his solo on B♭, the tonic note and principal pitch of the thematic riff.

Though connections to the head are understandably far less abundant in this more spontaneous venue, Parker is still *playing* "Lester Leaps

Ex. 3-9a: Wee (Head)

Ex. 3-9b: Wee - Solo Beginning

Ex. 3-9c: Wee - Solo Conclusion

In"—this is clear through much of the performance: Parker suggests the head by playing off its rhythm as heard in the band, treats it in sequence, then returns to it for inspiration throughout the remainder of his solo.

The B♭ rhythm-changes pieces sampled in this chapter have demonstrated structural relationships between Parker's solos and the original melodies in each case. Of the studio recordings, the weaker takes were often those in which the relationship to the original melody had not yet come into focus, although, as was seen in "Red Cross," excessive thematic reference can sometimes detract from the overall quality of the solo. Connection to the head was in evidence in the more extended live performances too, though perhaps not as consistently.

Not surprisingly, all the solos, being uptempo, were constructed largely through Parker's melodic formulas, but in many instances the formulas were relevant to the thematic material at hand. Relationships between Parker's solos and the original melodies were most often heard at higher structural levels, and through the abstraction of the foreground thematic material. Parker generally did not treat the thematic material in the manner of a development, with the possible exception of "Lester Leaps In," in which systematic references to the melodic riff dominated the latter half of the solo.

Parker, in effect, recalls the original melody *through* the connection of his motivic formulas, which are usually joined together to create foregrounds that seem quite similar on casual listening. The following two chapters of this study examine Parker's improvisations on standards and the blues to see if such relatedness is present there as well.

Chapter 4

Popular Song

Embraceable You

Parker's well-known "Embraceable You"[91] takes of October 28, 1947, are his only studio performances[92] of this ballad. The slow tempos enable Parker to embroider the middleground lines of the original melody with a multitude of diminutional ideas and motivic forms. For purposes of space, the analyses of these highly complex improvisations will be limited mostly to large-scale relationships with the original melody.[93]

Embraceable You—Original Melody

The original melody of "Embraceable You," shown in Ex. 4–1, is in classic 32-bar ABAC form.[94] In grasping the overall shape of the tune, it is helpful to compare the Schenkerian "interrupted" fundamental structure, which is in fact implied by many ABAC songs: the form is divided into two halves, mm. 1-16 and mm. 17-32; the first half typically ends on a half cadence, while the second half, after repeating the main thematic material from the first half, cadences to the tonic. In "Embraceable You," a $\hat{5}$-$\hat{4}$-$\hat{3}$-$\hat{2}$ // $\hat{5}$-$\hat{4}$-$\hat{3}$-$\hat{2}$-$\hat{1}$ fundamental line underlies the form, but with noteworthy complications. The melody rises to $\hat{5}$ at m. 7, but there is no $\hat{4}$ connecting to the $\hat{3}$ prolonged in mm. 9-12. In the second half, the $\hat{5}$ at m. 23 is followed by a clear $\hat{4}$-to-$\hat{3}$ descent in mm. 25-26.

The $\hat{5}$ as a primary tone receives special emphasis through the B4-natural in m. 14 and the D♭5 in m. 30, the only nondiatonic pitches in the melody. These two chromatic pitches not only point to $\hat{5}$ as the primary tone, but also serve to define the ends of each half. The resolution of D♭5 to C5 in the second half is only implied.

The melody is based on two principal motives, labeled X and Y in the example, which articulate two voice-leading lines in contrary motion. For example, the opening D4-F4 progresses to C4-G4, while the same

Ex. 4-1: Embraceable You (Melody)

idea, transposed up a fourth, defines the second phrase. At the melody's half cadence, in m. 15, the contrary motion encompasses an entire octave: G4 up to C5 and E4 down to C4. These octave C's are derived from a combination of Y and Y' — the low and high points of the first and second phrases. This idea is echoed at the end of the song with an expansion to E4-D♭5 contracting on the final pitch to F4 with implied C5.

Embraceable You—Take 1

Take 1 of "Embraceable You" is shown in Ex. 4–2. Parker's opening four bars are constructed by rearranging motives X and Y, as labeled in

Ex. 4-2: Embraceable You - Take 1

the sketch. This remarkable transformation of the song's opening motives also duplicates the original melody's initial centralizing of E4,
which appears on beat 3, and hence is stressed relative to the encircling
D4 and F4. Parker's opening motive also stresses E4, and surrounds it
from above (G4-F4-E4) and below (C4-D4-E4).

At the same time, the opening motive can be heard as derived through
the standard practice in bop of substituting extensions for more conso-
nant pitches: Parker's E4-G4 third can be heard as replacing the D4-F4
of the original melody—a substitution of the 7th and 9th for the 6th and
root. The same process follows in bars 3-4, where Parker's A4-C5 (9th

Ex 4-2: Embraceable You - Take 1

and 11th) can be heard as replacing G4-Bb4 (root and 3rd) from the tune's mm. 5-6.

Following the procedure of the original melody, Parker repeats his first bar, while adding embellishment. In mm. 3-4, Parker transposes his opening idea up a fourth—the same transposition used by the original melody in mm. 5-6. Similarly, just as the original melody's m. 6 repeats m. 5, Parker's m. 4 repeats m. 3—again, with embellishment. As a result

Ex. 4-2: Embraceable You - Take 1

of this procedure, Parker shortens his opening statement from six bars to four, while following the head's developmental process exactly.

Parker projects the C-G fifth in his opening phrase as motive Y. Upon transposition up a fourth in m. 3, however, the fifth is transformed to a C-D seventh, called Y''', that avoids the stark tonic implications of F-C in the original. Parker continues to avoid the thematically stable F-C fifth until m. 23, where its unfolding prepares the conclusion of the solo.

Ex 4-2: Embraceable You - Take 1

By compressing the first few bars, Parker articulates C5 as a primary tone of the fundamental line at m. 3—considerably earlier than its appearance in m. 7 of the head. As noted above, the C5 is an 11th of the Gm7 chord rather than an appoggiatura to the B♭4 in the same bar. In m. 5 the C5 does function locally as an appoggiatura to the B♭4, yet at a higher level it is prolonged throughout the first eight bars: note especially its appearance in m. 7, again as the 11th of Gm7, but then as the ♯11 of

G♭7. The C4 in m. 7 proceeds at the foreground to D4, so that m. 8 culminates with a hint of the D4-C5 seventh as motive Y′′′.

The $\hat{4}$ of the principal structural line, which is not present in the original melody's first half, is indeed articulated by Parker at m. 9 as an appoggiatura of the $\hat{3}$ on the "and" of beat 3. At this point, the original melody is quoted explicitly, with chromatic embellishments, suggested by the middleground lines of mm. 4-6. These embellishments foreshadow the descent to $\hat{2}$ in m. 12 (beats 3 and 4), and ultimately the descending chromatics of the solo's conclusion, mm. 28-33. The A4 in m. 9 is prolonged as $\hat{3}$ while the original melody's F-E is stated in diminution, notably throughout m. 9 and at the important harmonic change at m. 11. This is one of Parker's clearest uses of diminution, whereby an idea from the song itself is duplicated and reduplicated in various smaller-scale patterns.

The structural $\hat{2}$ at m. 12, on the "and" of beat 4, is also reinforced by the plaintive G5 of m. 13, as motive Y is composed out at this point in two registers. The G4-E4 third of the original melody provides another central idea for Parker's diminutions throughout mm. 13-14.

Parker's spacious octave C's in m. 15, are again taken directly from the original melody, which, at this point, also features the chromaticism B4-C5: Parker modifies this idea by transposing it down an octave and separating the pitches temporally. In the upper register, the B♭4 of m.15 and Parker's elegant run in m. 16 deflect attention from C5 until its reinstatement as the primary tone in m. 17.

As the second half begins, C5, the primary tone, is rearticulated without preparation in mm. 17-20. Parker also stresses E4 in mm. 17-18, paralleling its focus at this moment in the head. Motive Y is composed out in mm. 19-20, also paralleling its original treatment. In m. 21 the song's foreground surfaces briefly: whereas in the original, the G-B♭ third expands to the Y′ F4-C5 fifth at m. 23, Parker develops this idea further by composing out the F4-C5 fifth, then extending it in m. 24 to C5-F5. Thus, Parker delays explicit development of Y′, the tonic F-C fifth, until this rather late moment in the solo.

The structural line's $\hat{4}$ is articulated in two registers at m. 25. The C5-B♭4-A4 of the original melody in m. 25 appears in diminution, with chromatic motion through C♭5. Throughout mm. 26-27, Parker avoids A4, so that it will be a fresh and culminating note at m. 28. At m. 28, Parker again returns to the original melody quite explicitly.

Parker dramatically introduces the structural dominant $\hat{2}$ in m. 29 via the chromatic line A4 to A♭4 to G4. The G4 in m. 29 anticipates its higher-level rearticulation at m. 30, which interrupts the chromatic descent begun on A4 in m. 28. This small-scale interruption enables Parker to retrace the line in mm. 31-32, the second time with a resolution to F4 in m. 32. Parker subtly locates the solo's melodic resolution to F4 over the unstable Gmin7th and G♭maj7th harmonies, whereas at the harmonic resolution to F major in m. 33, Parker ends on the relatively unstable C4, thus recalling the F-C motive Y'.

In his concluding bars, Parker expands the use of the original melody's second chromaticism, D♭5-(C5), from single statement in mm. 29-30 to the composed-out central event of m. 30 and, in the lower register, the final phrase of the solo. Thus the interplay of D♭5-(C5), the climax of the original melody at m. 30, is extended by Parker to a single bar, then echoed as a final tag.

In the first take of "Embraceable You," Parker both derives his principal motives from the original melody and quotes parts of it directly. The middlegrounds between the solo and the original melody are often identical.

Take 1 may have influenced, however slightly, the motivic direction of take 2—the triplet figure at the downbeat of m. 10 is similar to the second take's main idea, for example. Further, the composed-out minor seventh intervals at the conclusion to take 1 virtually set up this important idea for take 2, so that, despite the decided difference in character between the takes, they could be heard jointly as an extended composition.

Embraceable You—Take 2

Though recorded immediately after take 1, take 2 (Ex. 4–3) features a considerably different motivic thrust and overall character.[95] Its diminutions are the equal of the first take's in ingenuity, but the overall performance is somewhat less sensitively conceived.

The essence of take 2's principal motive (C5-C4-D4 or F5-G4-B♭4, labeled M) is the interval of the minor seventh (labeled M'). Motive M is derived, albeit indirectly, from the original melody, as will become clear in the following discussion. Once stated at the downbeats of m. 1 and m. 4, motive M is composed out in a parallel manner in the first six bars: C5-A4-G4-*F4-D4* in mm. 1-3 is followed by F5-D5-C5-*B♭4-G4* in mm. 5-6; that is, the same transposition found in the original melody. The actual foregrounds that comprise these pair of descending minor-seventh chord lines are in themselves very different. Yet the minor thirds at the ends of these lines (D4-F4 and G4-B♭4) are motive M's link to the

Ex. 4-3: Embraceable You - Take 2

original melody. Motives M and M' also appear at the foreground through mm. 1-6.

As the thematic minor seventh, Motive M' forms the climactic phrase in m. 28, where it motivates the E5 and E♭5 rather than the original melody's A4. It also appears as the closing A3-G4 at m. 31 and as the coda-like figure that composes out G3-F4 in mm. 31-32. This latter figure duplicates the composing out of mm. 5-6. Parker's closing on 7̂ at m. 33 implies the resolution of the G3-F4 seventh in mm. 31-32 to the

Ex 4-3: Embraceable You - Take 2

(F3)-E4 seventh. The final D♭4-E4 recalls the significance of the D♭5 at m. 30 of the original melody. Hence, motive M, based on the minor seventh and derived from the original melody, is prominent at the beginning and ending of the take.

In addition to developing motive M, Parker composes out the original melody's voice-leading lines, as in take 1. Much of the middleground of Parker's solo reproduces the middleground of the original melody, ex-

cept that Parker begins with stating the primary tone $\hat{5}$ after a short pick-up rather than preparing it over several bars (as in the tune and in take 1). Directly articulating $\hat{5}$, motive M can be seen as derived from Parker's return, through the octave descent, to the more foreground aspects of the solo, that is, the original melody's D4-F4 third.

Of interest, too, is how Parker keeps the primary tone, C5, alive during mm. 3-6 (and, in parallel, during mm. 21-22): since this pitch is somewhat dissonant to the G4-B♭4 third (prolonged at a lower level from m. 4-6), Parker must *also* project C5. Once B♭4 is articulated at m. 4, the following run, though stressing both B♭4 and B♭3, hints artfully at C5 without disturbing the middleground B♭'s. Once m. 7 is reached, the C4, harmonized in simple F major, returns to the foreground together with the important F4 middleground pitch. With the support of the C4 in m. 7, the C5 can be now heard as prolonged from its initial statement in m. 1.

In the second half, the primary tone, C5, is accented adroitly in mm. 19-20, together with the lower-level B♭4. The B4-natural in m. 18 introduces the B♭4 in m. 19, but, in functioning as a neighbor to C5, helps keep the more background pitch alive. The C5 finally returns to foreground prominence at the height of the scale in mm. 23-24. Bar 23 recalls the pure F-major character of its corresponding first-half bar at m. 7.

Since Parker so often returns to fragments of the original melody, it could be argued that both takes of "Embraceable You" are enormously complicated paraphrases rather than improvisations on the original melody. This does not seem quite right, however, since the paraphrase, in concept, is closely based on and constrained by the original melody throughout — it is a more or less consistent ornamentation of that melody. The "Embraceable You" solos, by contrast, feature relational ingenuity of the highest order and many moments in which the original melody, while available in the background, is not being ornamented in the foreground. These are thematic improvisations, not paraphrases: the original material ingeniously and subtly directs the overall shape of the solo, but does not restrict or limit its melodic content.

Just Friends

The original melody of "Just Friends" has a single foreground element with obvious potential for thematic development, the descending tritone, yet Parker's studio solo[96] on this melody seems to ignore it completely. Parker works instead with material derived from a larger-scale view of the song's melodic structure. The sure-handed playing and especially deep affinities linking the solo to the original melody suggest that Parker's main ideas had been worked out beforehand — that the recording was accomplished in one take adds to the evidence.[97] After analysis of the original melody and the studio version, a fine solo recorded live, but with Parker improvising in a different key, will be examined for purposes of comparison.

Just Friends—Original Melody

The original melody of "Just Friends" (Ex.4–4) is in 32-bar ABAC form with an interrupted fundamental line. Besides suave harmonic changes, its most memorable characteristic, as noted above, is the descending-tritone, mm. 3, 7, 19, and 23, to unexpected chromaticisms supported by ♭VII7 and ♭VI7 chords.

Ex. 4-4: Just Friends (Melody)

A larger-scale feature of "Just Friends," in evidence throughout, is its use of descending seconds resolving to more stable pitches. The D5 at m. 1 and the C5 at m. 5 are appoggiaturas—sustained, as often the case in European practice, longer than their goal tones. Beginning on D5 in m. 1, and continuing to G4 in m. 12, these appoggiaturas and their resolutions articulate an important voice-leading line. The G4 in m. 12 motivates the G5 through octave transfer and also implies resolution to F4 at mm. 15-16, an implication alluded to by Parker in his solo.

The G♭4 and F♭4 (mm. 3 and 7) also imply resolutions and thereby create another key contrapuntal line of Parker's solo: G4 (implied, m. 1) proceeds to G♭4 (m. 3), followed by an F4 (implied, m. 5) to F♭4 (m. 7), to E♭4 (implied, m. 9), and lastly D4 (implied, m. 11). This latter pitch is the source, through octave transfer, of the D5's, mm. 12-15 and prolonged from m. 1 as the original melody's primary tone. The original D5-C5 motive returns to end the first half.

The second half of the melody duplicates the first half until the C5 in m. 26, at which point the cadence is prepared by backtracking to an (N-4)7 chord, D7, to initiate forward motion in the circle of fifths. The cadence, arriving in mm. 30-31, features a descent from F5, the 11th of the IImin7 chord, through D5 (the $\hat{3}$ of the basic structure) as the ♯9 of ♭II7 (the tritone substitute of the V7), before resolving to B♭4—$\hat{1}$ supported by the tonic.

The resolution pitch B♭4 at m. 31 is anticipated at m. 25, where it is prolonged through a double-neighbor until m. 28. Then at the middleground, the B♭4 rises to D5, supported by the structural dominant and prolonged since m. 17, before returning to conclude the song at m. 31. During the final prolongation of the D5 from m. 28 to m. 30, G5 and F5 recapitulate the basic motivic idea: descending seconds.

Just Friends—Studio Improvisation

Parker's studio improvisation of "Just Friends" (Ex. 4–5) is organized around two interrelated ideas: diminutional treatments of the descending-seconds motive and composing out the two implied voice-leading lines of the original melody.

The first phrase of the original melody proceeds D5-C5-G♭4. Parker follows this outline exactly, but at the same time elaborates it through diminutional techniques. Parker first resolves the motivic D5-C5 dyad of the original melody to B♭4 in m. 1. He then echoes the D5-C5-B♭4 a fifth below with G4-F4-E♭4 to complete the two-bar opening phrase. This transposi-

Ex. 4-5: Just Friends - Studio Solo

tion of the opening-third descent initiates the solo's two principal descending lines from D5 and G4 that duplicate those of the original melody.

Transposing D5-C5-Bb4 down a major third yields Bb4-Ab4-Gb4. Parker arrives at the thematic Gb4 at the end of m. 4 by composing out this Bb4-Ab4-Gb4 third through mm. 3-4. Hence the original D-C-Gb becomes D-C-Bb (mm. 1-2), then Bb-Ab-Gb (mm. 3-4). At a larger-scale level, the Gb4, prolonged through mm. 3-4, is now heard as proceeding

Ex 4-5: Just Friends - Studio Solo

from the G4 of m. 1. The motion from G4 to Gb4, implied but not articulated by the original melody, is a characteristic example of Parker fruc-
tifying the inherent possibilities of his thematic material.

Having established the two main voice-leading lines at the outset of
the solo, Parker proceeds to compose them out—the lower as G4 (m. 1),
Gb4 (m. 3), F4 (m. 5, accented and sustained), Fb4 (m. 8), Eb4 (m. 9), D4
(m. 11 and prolonged until m. 16) to C4 (m. 16). The upper line proceeds

Ex. 4-5: Just Friends - Studio Solo

from D5 (m. 1) to D♭5 in passing (m. 3) to C5 (m. 5) to B♭4 and A4 (m. 9) to G4 (m. 13) to F4 and F♯4 (m. 16).

Many of the diminutions in Parker's improvisation project the middleground lines through progressions of a third—as if Parker, having extended the original D5-C5 dyad to B♭4, were composing out and developing its larger-scale implications. Meanwhile, the two middleground lines themselves adumbrate the underlying structure of original melody.

The culmination of the upper voice-leading line at F♯4 in m. 16 sets up the lower voice-leading line's G4 in the second half of the solo. Parker completes the composing out of the lower line with D4-C4 in mm. 14-16 — in effect, transferring the motivic D5-C5 to the lower register. After the formal interruption of m. 16, both voice-leading lines are reinstated at their original registers for the solo's second half.

Parker, in the second half of his solo, continues to avoid obvious motivic material from the original melody, while still suggesting its principal features. These include the D5-C5 idea encapsulated in the fourth beat of m. 18, with again its extension to B♭4 (and G4); the near repeat of this figure in m. 19 (with the D5 and G4 flatted); the projection of C5-B♭4 in mm. 21-22; and the A4-B(♭)4-C5 alluded to ingeniously at the beginning and prolonged to the end of the phrase in mm. 27-28.

Yet, these foreground connections between the original melody and the solo continue to be less important than the diminutions of the two principal structural lines from G4 and D5. The lower line proceeds from G4 (m. 17) to G♭4 (mm. 19-20), F4 (m. 21), F♭4 (m. 23), E♭4 (m. 25), D4 (m. 26). The D4 is prolonged through to the end of the piece, eventually cadencing through C4 to B♭3. The upper line proceeds from D5 (m. 18) through D♭5 (m. 19) to C5 (m. 21) which is prolonged through to D5 in m. 29. The resolution to B♭4 is implied by octave transfer of the cadence in the lower register.

The pitch C5 is prolonged from m. 21 to m. 29 through double neighboring by D♭5 and B♭4, as in the first half. The especially skillful character of the second-half prolongation results from its lack of interruption by the cadence to G minor in m. 28 — C5 continues as an 11th of the G-minor harmony.

The lower principal line descends from G4, as in the first half, to D4 at m. 28. Progression to the cadential B♭3 occurs twice, the second being the structural resolution. The first D4-C4-B♭3 occurs supported by the G-minor harmony of m. 28; in m. 29 the D4 line at the middleground reaches back to E4, and after a chromatic return to D4, finally closes to B♭3 in m. 31. The D-to-B♭ third progression in the meantime also appears in diminution — for example, in the first beat of m. 28, from the end of m. 29 to the second beat of m. 30, within the fourth beat of m. 30, and finally in the very last two pitches of the solo.

Parker's artistry in suggesting indirect connections to the original melody is especially evident on the "Just Friends" studio take. Working primarily with the principal structural lines and descending seconds, he creates an unexpected enlargement of the original melody's motivic structure. The more obvious foreground references to the original are hidden in a complex of elegant diminutions. With its reworking of the thematic material inventive, ingenious, yet subtle, this recording must rank among Parker's most satisfying improvisations.

Just Friends—Café Society ("Pop")

In addition to the studio version, seven live performances of "Just Friends" were recorded by Parker under more informal circumstances. Five are with strings, using the same arrangement as the studio version, and two are with a small combo. For the small-group versions, Parker improvises on the melody in A♭ rather than B♭.[98]

The live performances with strings duplicate many of the thematic ideas found in the studio improvisation. Parker, for example, always begins with the studio version's opening motive, or some slight variant. Though in many ways these recordings are excellent, Parker generally follows much of the studio version's voice-leading plan and thematic structure.[99]

The two performances recorded at the Café Society are distinguished from the "with strings" versions, however, in both motivic structure and voice-leading plan. In the one chosen for this study ("Pop"—Ex. 4–6),[100] Parker quotes "Pop Goes the Weasel" at m. 31. Since, for these performances, the group remains entirely in A♭, Parker avoids the thematic structures of the B♭ improvisations and instead connects to the original in a wholly different manner.

The C-B♭ motivic dyad (labeled Y in Ex. 4–6) from the original melody[101] appears in mm. 1-2 and forms an integral part of the solo's motivic surface. It resurfaces an octave higher in mm. 5-6, mm. 9-10, mm. 12-13, is strongly articulated at the beginning of the second half in mm. 17-18, and is highlighted in the run of m. 25. Frequently, motive Y is conjoined to A♭, as in mm. 5-6 and mm. 12-13. A critical use of motive Y, which recalls the start of the solo, is found in m. 33, as if topping off the improvisation.

Similarly, the conspicuous F♭ from the original melody appears in configuration with its resolution tone E♭—which was only implied in the original melody—in m. 3, mm. 4-5, m. 20, and mm. 20-21. Thus, at least two prominent dyads from the head are featured at the foreground of the solo as well. Important step-wise dyads other than C-B♭ (motive Y) are labeled Y′.

An ingenious network of motivic connections culminates in the

Ex. 4-6: Just Friends - Café Society "Pop"

climactic G5's at mm. 14 and 29. The G5's appear with F5's (motive Y'), while the F5-C5 fourth that completes the figure is found at m. 14 and (in modified form) mm. 29-30 of the original melody. Parker leads to the climactic G5-F5-C5 motive via the D♭5-F♭5-C♭5 ideas of m. 7 and m. 8. This idea in turn is derived from the opening C4-A♭3-B♭3 which serves to introduce motive Y. Measures 3-4 are derived from the opening statement of motive Y as well. Thus the source of Parker's main motivic ideas and improvisational highpoints can be located clearly in the thematic descending dyads and climaxes of the original melody.

Ex. 4-6: Just Friends - Café Society "Pop"

Despite these foreground references, the principal game plan of the solo, as in the studio performance, is the composing out of key middle-ground lines derived from the original melody. This solo, however, alters the original melody's middleground lines rather than repeating them: in place of an interrupted-form plan, this solo accumulates momentum by building to a strong projection of the pitch C5 at the beginning of the second half.

Hence, the motivic crux of the solo from the middleground point of view is the E♭4-C5 sixth at m. 5. The E♭4 is introduced by the descending line from A♭4, the solo's pickup, while the C5, on the other hand, initiates a new register and is introduced through a skip at the foreground from E♭4 and at the middleground from the initial A♭4.

Parker treats the interval of the sixth, the shape of the E♭4-C5 motive thematically. Key instances of it are bracketed in the transcription, such as the A♭4-C4 of the opening phrase, the leap from A♭4 to F♭5 in m. 6, the descending D♭5-E4 of m. 15, A♭4-F♭5 in m. 19, D♭5-F♭5 in m. 20, and E♭5-G♭4 in m. 23. Further, the interval of the sixth is composed out as E4-D♭5 (twice) in m. 27, E4-G3 in m. 27, and D♭4-F3 in mm. 27-28. The D♭5-E4 in m. 29 repeats the motivic idea of m. 15. The solo's concluding gesture (m. 33) repeats C4-A♭4 from m. 1.

Despite the middleground progression from C5 to B♭4 between mm. 5-10, C5 is prolonged at the background throughout the first half to m. 17. At this point, the lower middleground line has risen from E♭4 (m. 5) to F4 (m. 13), so that the two voice-leading lines from the original melody are articulated at the beginning of the second half.

Progression from C5-F4 in m. 17 now takes place in a manner reminiscent of the voice-leading lines of the original melody. At the middleground, C5 descends only as far as A♭4, much as in the first half (A♭4 there at m. 13; in the second half at m. 28). At the background, C5 is prolonged throughout the entire improvisation, ultimately to the structural dominent in m. 30. Since the lower line has by now returned to E♭4, the original E♭4-C5 sixth has been rearticulated for resolution to the tonic at m. 31. Hence, the solo recomposes the original melody's voice-leading lines: an interrupted form is transformed into a more through-composed setting.

The inclusion of "Pop Goes the Weasel" at m. 31 seems to mock the cadence to A♭ major—as if the C5, propped up at the background since m. 5, is yielding to an anticlimactic A♭4.[102] Yet after the resolution to the tonic, Parker's addendum in mm. 32-33 converges on and highlights the motivic A♭4-C4-(A♭3)-B♭3 in a structurally illuminating final flourish, as if to say that the solo is indeed serious.

Furthermore, "Pop Goes the Weasel" does indeed fit, if in a trivial sense, the thematic structure of the improvisation: the C5-A♭4 (beat three to beat four) recapitulates the solo's large-scale background line, the final E♭5-C5-A♭4 triplet duplicates the final three notes of the original melody, and the rising A♭4-B♭5-C5 line that leads to this figure is rhythmically grouped in dyads that recall the initial A♭4 to C5 from the pickup to m. 5. Most importantly, the key E♭4-C5 sixth encloses the quotation.

The Café Society "Pop" performance is a superb effort, emotionally appealing and informed by subtle structural interconnection—even "Pop Goes the Weasel" is embedded, though distantly, in the thematic texture. The foreground motives of the original melody are more prevalent here than in the studio version, perhaps because of the greater spontaneity of the performance venue, and because Parker was already accustomed to playing the head in this key. The solo's greater angularity, aggressiveness, and off-handedness probably derive from the lack of string support and the live, small-group setting.

Cherokee and Koko

Among Parker's most famous recordings is the classic "Koko" of 1945,[103] with changes based on the structure of "Cherokee."[104] The long note values of "Cherokee" might seem at first glance to have little to do with the agile, virtuosic masterpiece of 1945, but the melody almost certainly influenced structural aspects of Parker's solo. Indeed, the false start of take 1 contains part of the melody of "Cherokee," so we know the musicians at first intended to play the original.

"Cherokee" had been a featured solo for Parker in the McShann band. There is an informal recording of "Cherokee" made probably in 1942 at Monroe's with Parker accompanied (probably) by the house band.[105] Parker's 1942 improvisation can be heard as an earlier version of the well-known Savoy recording—it shows Parker's approach to this tune as a virtual work in progress.

Example 4–7a aligns the first half of the bridge of "Cherokee" with the Monroe's first bridge and the Savoy first bridge. Notice that the Monroe's bridge follows the original melody quite closely and is highly sequential. The Savoy first bridge, played about three years later, further develops the Monroe's solo by reducing the too-mechanical effect of its sequences through the addition of extra space and a freer overall melodic line. The latter solo reflects Parker's growing maturity and the stylistic development of the bop line itself, yet both bridges are derived from the original melody.

The A sections are rather less dependent on the original tune. But surely this might be expected, since the difficult, tonally distant II-V-I's of the bridge were probably the source of the tune's initial appeal to the bop players. Nonetheless, the A sections do reveal some thematic connection to the original melody. For example, the Savoy version has a the-

Ex. 4-7a - Cherokee / Koko Bridges

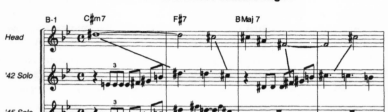

matic idea of its own, the melody of the opening three bars (Ex. 4–7b),
which is repeated exactly at the beginning of the second A section. It returns in slightly altered form in the last A section of the solo.

The opening idea of Parker's Savoy solo is related to the original
melody of "Cherokee," moreover: for in the original, the third and fourth
bars contain B♭4 and G4, respectively the 9th and 13th of the Fm7 and
B♭7 chords (examples of the upper extensions already contained in the
melody). In Parker's transformation, the B♭4 and G4 are altered to B♭4
and F♯4, creating a "be-bop" modification of the extended-chord tones
heard in the original thematic material (Ex. 4–7b).

There is even a secondary idea: the triplets in mm. 1A1-5 to 1A1-8
(Ex. 4–7c, top staff). This idea also returns in varied form in Parker's final A section, after the repeat of the original motivic idea (Ex. 4–7c, bottom staff).

Thus, Parker's solo on "Koko" is based on thematic ideas derived
from the original melody of "Cherokee," and is organized as a statement
of thematic material, its development, then a return to that material in the
final A3 section. The very conclusion of the solo suggests a $\hat{3}$-$\hat{2}$-$\hat{1}$ fundamental line that duplicates the fundamental line of the tune, thus relating
the solo to its original source material even more closely.

Parker's modifications of "Cherokee" can be heard in embryonic form in the Monroe's version, but the relatedness to the original melody is more convincing in the Savoy version. In all probability, Parker gradually derived his recomposition of the original through numerous performances that eventually culminated in the Savoy recording.[106] The studio version, in view of its brilliance and pervasive influence in jazz history, can be considered definitive although Parker recorded the tune live several times afterwards with continuing evolution of the thematic material.

Star Eyes

The Verve studio session of "Star Eyes"[107] features a Parker solo sensitively rendered—a beautiful performance of this standard. Aural references to the theme abound not only in the solo, but also at the beginning of the recording (ex. 4–8a), which shows the characteristic dyads of the theme reversed in the introductory figure. Other thematic references—including Parker's first improvised phrase (Ex. 4–8b), the beginning of the bridge (Ex. 4–8c), and the conclusion of the solo (Ex. 4–8d)—are unmistakable. Note especially the very ending of Parker's solo, where his last two notes refer directly to the tune, while not duplicating it in any obvious manner. Despite the clarity of the references, the solo, like the

Ex. 4-7b: Koko First Idea

Ex. 4-7c - Koko Secondary Idea

"Embraceable You" performances, should not be considered a para-phrase.

Live performances of "Star Eyes" also incorporate extensive refer-ences to the original melody. For example, the performance at the St. Nicholas Arena,[108] which includes a "Pop Goes the Weasel" quotation on the restatement of the head, is similar to the Verve studio version in containing numerous thematic references. Many of its diminutions are based clearly on the longer note values heard in the original melody. To

Ex. 4-8a: Star Eyes Introduction

Ex. 4-8b: Star Eyes Studio Opening

Ex. 4-8c: Star Eyes Studio Bridge

cite but a single instance, ex. 4–8e shows a slightly less obvious reference based on an adroitly executed octave transfer.

As in Parker's rhythm-changes improvisations, his solos on more popularly-based material reveal frequent and sophisticated references to the theme. The lyrical nature of "Embraceable You" and "Star Eyes" is especially well adapted to explicit references to the original melody, but neither of these solos, especially the latter, should be construed as paraphrase: rather, much of their thematic interest is based on very subtle examples of reference rather than the overt ornamentation typical of ballad performance. "Just Friends" is an intermediate case between popular-song performance and an outright bop tune: uptempo but explicitly intended for popular listening (given the song itself and the strings accompaniment), it features an improvisation that ranks among Parker's most successful, both as self-contained composition and as recomposition of the original material.

Ex. 4-8d: Star Eyes Studio Ending

Ex. 4-8e: Star Eyes Live

The solos on "Cherokee" and "Koko" are rather more like the rhythm-changes solos examined earlier: with a jazz-tune, "blowing" character, they are more removed from the original melody, despite occasional instances of thematic reference. Both solos veered toward the development of self-contained thematic material, too, particularly "Koko," yet thematic reference could be found nevertheless.

Thus, as with the rhythm-changes solos, Parker will often allude to the head in his popular-song improvisations. Not surprisingly, in most cases the references are even more explicit.

Chapter 5

The Blues

The blues[109] differs from the popular-song and jazz-tune repertoires in two principal respects: first, it is less functional harmonically—given that its chord changes less often invoke patterns derived from the circle of fifths. Second, blue-note effects, riffs, and greater reliance on melodic formulas associate the music more closely with the African element of the jazz stylistic genesis.[110] The riffs most especially—rhythmic melodic patterns repeated over shifting harmonies—may weaken harmonic function, principally when the patterns are not suitably altered to follow the changes.

Thematic relatedness in Parker's rhythm-changes and popular-song improvisations is sometimes coupled to harmonic progression—for example, in those instances when the harmonic function of a given melody or of some melodic motive derived from it influences the solo.[111] It seems quite reasonable to suspect that in the blues, there may be fewer such connections, given the (usually)[112] less functional nature of the genre.

Blues *characteristically* features recurring formulas—not only within a given artist's work but also throughout the genre as an overall defining quality. Indeed, since common-currency blues formulas are so widespread and so frequently become clichés, it would seem that convincing motivic relatedness to the head would virtually be precluded on this basis alone. An especially clear example of a melodic formula heard in numerous Parker blues choruses is Owens's M. 10a, as shown in Ex. 5–1. The syncopated ♭3 is the blue third of the key and flat seven of the IV7 chord. This motive will be heard on various solos referred to in this section, and is an especially apt instance of a Parker formula that could be introduced in virtually any blues performance irrespective of thematic consequence.

Yet, as was shown in earlier chapters, Parker, while usually instilling a great number of motivic formulas into his solos, still manages to associate

Ex. 5-1: Blues Formula (Owens M. 10a)

with the head, however indirectly — and to this end blues heads often feature poignant melodic ideas, which may factor thematically in Parker's
improvisations despite possible status as blues clichés. Hence it is possible that a sense of thematic relatedness may still typify Parker's work
on the blues, but that the relatedness may be somewhat more indirect, as
observed from time to time in several of the rhythm-changes solos. In order to gain a sense of the motivic connection of blues heads to Parker solos, let us conclude the analytical portion of this study with brief comments on a cross-section of recordings in this area, beginning first with
a somewhat more extensive comparison between two sets of C major
blues, "Cool Blues" and "Perhaps."

Cool Blues

"Cool Blues"[113] epitomizes riff-like blues construction, for its entire
melody comprises the phrase shown in Ex. 5–2a played three times over
the standard harmonic paradigm of the 12-bar blues. (Parker usually flats
the first E4 the second time through in order to align the riff harmonically with F7.) The first part of the riff emphasizes the pitch G4, which
is encircled from the bottom from E4 and the top from C5. The triplet
beginning the riff will be called motive A. Perhaps the most memorable
quality of the riff is its cadence to D4, the ninth (or second) of the key,
which is called B, and is an instance of a more general (non-motivic) thematic pattern. The large-scale structure of the riff shows progression
from G4 to E4 — an augmentation and abstraction of motive A, as again
labeled in the example.

Take 1 begins with a flatted variant of motive A, rhythmicized into bluesy triplets (Ex. 5–2b). The syncopated ending of the first phrase, though cadencing on C4 rather than D4, recalls the rhythm of the thematic riff. The figure leading to the fifth bar of the first chorus is the Parker formula, Owens's M. 10a,[114] mentioned above. In the second chorus of take 1, thematic pattern B (the cadence to D4) is also alluded to in m. 2-6 (Ex. 5–2c)—perhaps to avoid formula M. 10a. In this case the E is also flatted, so it is labeled as B′. The second chorus also clearly outlines motive A as its large-scale structure.

Take 2 begins with commensurate emphasis of motive A, as in the thematic riff (Ex. 5–2d). The pitch D4 (thematic pattern B) is especially prominent: it is highlighted as part of the improvisational line, which, in conjunction with motive A, closely recalls the theme, while at no time duplicating it in any obvious manner. Throughout the take motive A is featured. The solo trails off with a final recollection of the important pitch, G4.

Take 3 (Ex. 5–2e) is much slower—apparently a concession to pianist Erroll Garner,[115] who was uncomfortable with the brighter tempos of the first two takes. Motive A, in its larger-scale, more abstract form as a G4-E4 succession, dominates the melodic fabric here more directly than in the second take.

Take 4, like the first take, is motivically more independent of motive A than the second and third takes. However, the three cited bars (Ex. 5–2f) show cadences to D4 or D5, the thematically prominent pitch in the original riff.

It could be claimed that Parker's better solos on "Cool Blues" are those in which he is thematically least reliant on the the structures of the riff. That is, takes 1 and 4 are the more inspired, and as such they feature less overt use of G4-E4. The weakest take, number 3, seems bound to motive A, as if Parker were unable to strike out freely on his own. Nonetheless, all the takes recall the riff in ways that tie the solos to it thematically—though, with the exception of the prominent use of D4 in take 2 (Ex. 5–2d), the references are less convincing than those examined in earlier chapters.

It is quite possible that a riff-like head may be a less powerful source of thematic reference more generally; a more distant relationship was also noted with "Lester Leaps In," as described in Ch. 3. For in riff-like themes, not only is there less material to work with, but their repetitive nature would seem to impel the soloist to apply contrasting ideas as a counterbalance. Even in "Lester Leaps In," for example, Parker returns to the theme only late in the solo.

Ex. 5-2a: Cool Blues Head

Ex. 5-2b: Cool Blues Take 1 (Start)

Ex. 5-2c: Cool Blues Take 1 (m. 2-5)

Ex. 5-2d: Cool Blues Take 2 (Start)

Ex. 5-2e: Cool Blues Take 3 (Start)

Ex. 5-2f: Cool Blues Take 4 Excerpts

Perhaps

"Perhaps"[116] is another C blues, recorded about a year and a half later than "Cool Blues," and as such offers good ground for thematic comparison, for there is both sufficient distance from the earlier recording and useful temporal proximity as well. The head differs in style considerably from "Cool Blues," which consisted of a single repeated riff. The recording session for this tune was difficult for Parker in that he experienced problems with squeaking—hence, the need for seven takes.[117]

"Perhaps" is thematically richer than "Cool Blues," and, accordingly, yields Parker more potential for thematic reference. The tune (Ex. 5–3a) is especially noteworthy in its large-scale structure: a prolonged G4, established at the outset, then reclaimed by a gradual chromatic descent from C5 in m. 5 through mostly extended-chord tones: B4 (♯11 of F7) in m. 6, B♭4 (♭9 of A7) in m. 8, A4 (fifth of Dm) in m.9, A♭4 (♭9 of G7or fifth of D♭7) in m. 9, to G4 as the last note of the tune. Significant motives X and Y are labeled as well in the example.

Immediately upon hearing take 1, we find in the first chorus the salient thematic point seized upon by Parker throughout the session: the figure beginning in m. 1-9, motive X, which leads to the cadence of the chorus. This figure is transcribed at the start of Ex. 5–3b; instances of motive-X variants from other takes are compiled in the remainder of the example.

The Parker blues formula (Owens's M. 10a), discussed above in the section on "Cool Blues," is heard in take 1, at m. 1-5. It recurs in the third chorus. This Parker formula is so pervasive in his blues work (usually to introduce the IV chord in m. 5) that often it seems as if Parker were trying to find new ways of either avoiding the figure or extending it in some unexpected way. Such a felicitous development of this figure can be heard in take 3. After avoiding M. 10a in the first chorus at m. 1-5, Parker, in the second chorus, m. 2-5, embeds the figure in a longer line, as shown in Ex. 5–3c; further, this extended line reaches to B4, the ♯11 of the F7 chord, which was featured in the original melody (Ex. 5–3a) at roughly this same point. Finally, in m. 2-10, Parker refers to motive X in double time—perhaps his most interesting extension of *that* basic thematic unit as well (Ex. 5–2b).

Take 3, in m. 2-8, also includes a hesitating reference to what is called motive Y in the original melody. This concluding motive, a rising line that Koch equates with the tune's title (1988, 136), is echoed by Parker at several points in these takes, most notably in take 7, mm. 1-10 and 1-11, and at the very end of this same take, as shown in Ex. 5–3d.

In the last two complete takes, 6 and 7, not only does Parker incorporate the thematic references noted in the last paragraph, but he also begins fragmenting his references to motive X. (These references were summarized in Ex. 5–3b.) It may be that Parker considered the clear-cut references to the theme to be too obvious, or that he was tiring of the longer variants and trying to come up with something new.

In sum, it seems clear that "Cool Blues" and "Perhaps," both uncomplicated blues themes in C major, feature solos that *do* differ among themselves thematically with relation to their respective heads. That

Ex. 5-3a: Perhaps Head

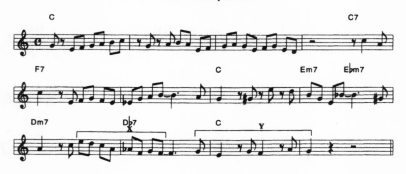

Ex. 5-3b: Perhaps Motive X Variants

"Perhaps" features both more and more ingenious thematic reference should not be surprising, given its greater thematic potential. Takes 2 and 6 of "Perhaps" are the strongest musically of that set, despite the problems with squeaks, in part because of their cogent references to the theme. The "Cool Blues" takes are slightly less rich with respect to thematic reference; but despite Parker's possible discomfort with Garner's presence on the tune, even there he manages connections to its identifying riff, within the context of blues choruses that should be considered first-rate irrespective of thematic content.

Ex. 5-3c: Embedded Formula and Theme in Take 3

Ex. 5-3d: Thematic Hesitations in Take 7

With "Cool Blues" and "Perhaps" as models of thematic reference to be found in Parker's blues material, the following presents a summarizing overview of other blues recordings in which similar kinds of thematic reference can be cited.

Au Privave

The original melody of "Au Privave"[118] features a motive, M, outlining a fourth from F4 to C4 (Ex. 5–4). (The melody also culminates on a variant of this motive in its cadence to F5 in m. 10 [not shown in the example].) The first chorus of Parker's solo evokes another motive, Y, from the original melody (m. 1-2) and ends with a simplification of M (m. 1-11). The second chorus begins with M displaced rhythmically by a beat (m. 1-12). The solo ends with motive M, again simplified, as its final two notes (m. 5-1).

Blues for Alice

"Blues for Alice"[119] (Ex. 5–5) is based on the circle of fifths, but retains the overall harmonic outline of the standard 12-bar blues. Parker's second chorus reproduces much of the material from the head: the first four

bars are strikingly similar—retracing the overall path of the original, but
with its melody distinctively recomposed.

Bongo Bop

The head of "Bongo Bop"[120] has a fundamental structural line of $\hat{5}$-$\hat{4}$-$\hat{3}$-
($\hat{2}$)-$\hat{1}$. (The $\hat{2}$ is more an appoggiatura to the final 1 than a structural pitch.)
Parker's second chorus on take 2 also follows this structure. Further, the
original melody is unified through a series of motivic forms marked X
and shown in the top staff of Ex. 5–6. Parker's second take hints at variants of X, as also shown in the example, on the second staff.

Ex. 5-4: Au Privave

Ex. 5-5: Blues for Alice

Ex. 5-6: Bongo Bop

Now's the Time

The main idea of "Now's the Time,"[121] labeled T, articulates a C4-F4 fourth, with neighboring motions from F4 to G4 and A♭4, and from C4 to B♭3 and B3 (Ex. 5–7). The sketch in the example also shows the large-scale prolongation of C4-F4 with the associated neighbor motions. The pitches D4 and E♭4 filling in the fourth are reserved for the last four bars of the melody before its conclusion on B3, the bebop flat 5. Parker's solo (one of his last studio sessions) highlights F-C fourths and fifths in numerous ways that recall the original melody's basic structure.[122] Excerpts are shown in the bottom three staves of the example.

Cheryl

The relationship between solo and head in "Cheryl"[123] is created through prolongation of G4, especially through neighbor motion to A4 (Ex. 5–8—these pitches are connected with curved lines). Parker's culminating third chorus, transcribed fully in the example, evokes this structural quality of the original melody.

The quotation of "Cool Blues" at the start of Parker's third chorus of "Cheryl" is especially apt—even thematic—since, as was shown above, the pitch G4 was a defining quality of "Cool Blues." (Note that the D4 is less emphasized by the riff in this—its quoted version—since Parker does not linger on the pitch or follow it with a substantial pause. Compare its earlier use in the opening of "Cool Blues," take 2, above.) Thus the quotation is not an extraneous feature of the solo.[124]

Parker's Mood

Let us conclude the analyses with a consideration of "Parker's Mood,"[125] one of his best-known blues recordings, but one without a (12-bar) theme at all. The identity of the recording is established from the outset with an out-of-tempo introductory figure (functioning outside the strophic 12-bar choruses) that returns at the end of take 5 (the master) as coda (Ex. 5–9a). The underlying idea of this signature motive is a large-scale progression from D5 to C5, as bracketed in the example. Throughout the second, fourth, and fifth takes of the solo,[126] this basic structure is evoked

through numerous D-C elaborations, which are modified to D♭-C on subdominant chords (D♭ providing the 7th of E♭7).

The finest performance of "Parker's Mood" is on the master take,
which features D-C and D♭-C melodic ornamentation to a greater extent
than the earlier efforts. Example 5–9b shows the last seven bars of
Parker's concluding chorus (after the piano solo) where the D-C motions
are bracketed. Especially evocative is Parker's concluding figure, before
the return of the introductory motive as coda: a *D4*-(B♭3)-*C4* triplet
(m. 12 in the example), whose relation to the signature motive (to follow) is readily apparent. Finally, the decision to include the introductory

Ex. 5-9a: Parker's Mood - Intro Motive

Ex. 5-9b: Parker's Mood - Concluding Chorus

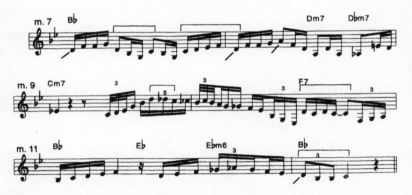

figure[127] as coda in the final take creates a more unified structure for the performance overall.[128]

From the sampling of solos examined in this section, it seems reasonable to conclude that thematic reference typifies Parker's blues playing, and that the nature of the reference is similar to the usages cited in the other two major genres of his improvising style. That is, even in the blues — unique among the stylistic genres for its close associations with the African origins of jazz — Parker's thematic procedures seem consistent, not at all unlike what was observed in rhythm changes or more popularly based material. Hence, whether Parker is playing the blues, jazz heads, or popular songs, thematic connection to the original melody will often unify the performances. In the final chapter, the nature of thematic reference in improvisation will be explored further and, with reference to Parker, placed in historical context.

Chapter 6

Master Soloist

General Style Considerations

The outstanding, perhaps the defining, quality of Parker's treatment of thematic relationships is his balance of melodic formula, especially in uptempo playing, with larger-scale voice leading and control that artfully evoke the original material. That is, Parker's melodic formulas[129] are re-worked from solo to solo with the head directly and indirectly motivating larger-scale concerns. The formulas themselves vary from pervasive, small-scale fragments to larger, multi-measure phrases. The original material is rarely developed in systematic fashion; instead, Parker alludes to its thematic patterns through various combinations of abstraction, diminution, voice-leading finesses, and so forth. These connections particularize the solo; hence familiar small-scale material can reappear throughout the Parker oeuvre without jeopardizing the uniqueness of the improvisation. (As particularly germane to this study as well as connecting to larger-scale issues in both Parker's style and jazz more generally, formula will be discussed in further detail after this summary of Parker's style.)

Voice-leading analysis has shown throughout that Parker's improvised line implies an almost continuous three- to five-part polyphony. As in Bach's compound melodies, the voice-leading implications of the line are meticulously attended to. Small-scale resolutions are customary; yet whenever pitches are unresolved or registers abandoned, they are usually taken up later in the solo, often for significant structural or dramatic purpose.[130] Alongside this pervasive unfolding of rich, contrapuntal textures, Parker often increases suspense and creates complexity by delaying structural tones through elaborate and ingenious ornamentation.[131] At the same time, he will seem to juggle the implied voice-leading lines through frequent accents and ghosted notes, which, in shifting the listener's attention rapidly from one implied line to another, create the overall effect of a contrapuntal whirlwind.

The hocket-like interplay of the voice-leading parts also reinforces the confident, aggressive character of Parker's line. Hocket-like texture can also be observed in the note-to-note contrast of ghosted and accented pitches, which propels Parker's foreground line, in uptempo playing, with an unparalleled sense of swing. The line, moreover, is usually "on top of the beat"—perhaps just slightly ahead of the rhythm section.[132] More driving passages are often counterbalanced by holding back, playing "behind the beat"—to create a relaxed, almost cadencing quality, which, as a result, intensifies the vibrancy of the uptempo lines through dramatic contrast.

Parker's line is further enhanced through irregular phrasing and through its large-scale syncopation with respect to the eight-bar symmetries and customary harmonic rhythms of the song forms. His phrasing and accents will sometimes cut across the grain of these symmetries, but as often as not, he is content to conform to the song form by generally not phrasing across its sectional divisions. *Within* each sectional division, however, Parker's phrasing often creates a vivid counterpoint to the regularity of the 2- and 4-bar harmonic rhythms, which arise from the symmetries of the song form itself.[133]

The general melodic direction of Parker's phrases tends to be downward. For example, a highpoint may be articulated, with or without preparation, followed by a gradual descent. It is quite likely that Parker's careful attention to voice leading partly accounts for his lines' overall downwards direction, since chromatic voice leading in circle-of-fifths patterns proceeds in such a manner normatively.[134]

Voice-leading analysis of Parker's work also helps reveal an especially effective device for generating elaborate and unexpected diminutions: Parker will often establish a higher-register pitch as a structural tone at some level, and follow it with a downwards-moving line in (usually) smaller note values, then return to rearticulate the structural tone for progression as a larger-scale motion. Such a procedure, which is especially common in his ballad playing, creates exquisite diminutional complexity and richness. Moreover, in ballad playing this kind of technique, applied more directly, can result in paraphrase of the original tune, with its longer note values providing structural supports for interpolated diminutions. Parker, not surprisingly, uses this technique both in paraphrasing the original tune and in referring to it within more freely constructed improvisation.

While it is apparent that Parker approaches improvisation harmonically, through constant attention to and articulation of the changes, his bop-style chordal innovations were originally scorned by more conservative listeners as unpleasantly dissonant. In hindsight, such antipathy to Parker's extended-chord tones is rather surprising, given that Parker invariably resolves them to pitches with greater harmonic support. That is, Parker's style, though adventurous in numerous respects, is firmly rooted in the Western tradition of voice leading based on triadic consonance. Indeed, throughout the voice-leading analyses of the studio work examined in the earlier chapters, there seems to be no time when Parker did not resolve extended-chord tones to more stable pitches. Peculiar resolutions, or even total nonresolutions, are surely to be heard in longer, more experimental performances, but when Parker was recording for dissemination among the public, he carefully attended to the tonal implications of his melodic lines. Parker in this sense is a musical conservative, a caretaker of the tonal tradition, which, with jazz adaptations, finds its original inspiration more in the musical outlook of a Bach than of a Cage.

In contrast to Parker's experimental work in harmonic extensions, his written compositions show relative lack of interest in unusual chord progressions or innovation of musical form. For among Parker's 49 original compositions, all are written in standard songforms and only six have original changes. Even of these six, three are quite closely related to pre-existing harmonic models.[135] We can account for this close reliance on the existing tradition by suggesting that Parker preferred the "blowing" chord patterns[136] of the regular songforms so that he could focus on what truly fascinated him—rhythmic/melodic innovation coupled to extensions and substitutions of familiar harmonies—without having to cope with the confusions of entirely new material. Further, Parker composed much of his work for hastily arranged recording sessions, so it became even more important that his pieces were readily accessible and so based on the standard changes. Most significantly, within the oral jazz tradition which was largely Parker's own, written experimentation and extension were simply not desiderata: what counted most was the immediate effect of the music, spontaneously produced, on the listener.

Nonetheless, Parker was an important innovator within the limits presented by the jazz tradition of his time. In addition to outstanding rhythmic innovation, his obsessive explorations of upper extensions and standard chord patterns—the latter reconfigured through imaginative and functional substitutions—were of the utmost importance in the development of bop style from swing.

Quotation

Parker's quotation of unrelated melodies within improvised solos is a well-known feature of his style, which has had a telling effect on other jazz players. The best quotations are often quite clever and function exquisitely in context. Exemplified by the appearance of "Cool Blues" in "Cheryl" (Ex. 5–8), such a quotation does not undermine the mood or deflect attention from the solo's main thrust. It is deftly woven into the thematic plan of the improvisation, complements its overall character, and does not dilute its emotional import.[137] A long-time jazz tradition, recognizable tunes unexpectedly appearing in an otherwise complex improvisation can amuse without necessarily trivializing. They also afford both player and listener a few seconds respite from assessing the more complex qualities of the solo.

Many times, Parker's quotations seem more ad hoc, more of a spontaneous reaction to personal events or the unpredictable circumstances of live performance milieus. In other words, such quotations usually occur under more relaxed performing conditions—and especially in more extended playing. Parker is usually discreet with unrelated quotations when recording professionally; here the result would be scrutinized and heard repeatedly, so he is understandably somewhat more careful. Further, with only one or two choruses of playing time available, a quotation is more intrusive and might deflect the listeners' consideration from other aspects of the solo.

All in all, Parker's quotations, whether live or in the studio, can function as clever additions to the overall performance. Some quotations may pass by the listener unnoticed, though their melodic simplicity will usually call attention to themselves in some way, even if the listener does not recognize the tune. When they are clearly intended as humorous asides,[138] they contribute an off-hand, mood-lightening quality to the improvisation. Quotations have long been an informal aspect of the jazz improvisation.[139] Under the best circumstances, they are entertaining and well-integrated into the solo; at other times, their informality and spontaneity require that we not evaluate them too seriously.

Other Issues in Thematic Reference

Parker's recorded solos sometimes appear without a head functioning as a source of thematic reference. As mentioned in Ch. 2, the theme was often omitted to allow more space for the solo, while at other times the practice obviated copyright payments to the composer and publisher. A third scenario, a kind of half measure, can be cited in "Parker's Mood"[140] in which, while there is no theme as such, the introductory figure identifies the piece and provides a thematic pattern identifiable in the solo.

When the head is unstated—for example, in Parker's "Koko"[141]—relationship to the original thematic material, if it exists, is complex. Three scenarios can be cited: (1) the solo contains no thematic references; (2) the solo might refer thematically to some (unstated) jazz head; or (3) the solo might refer thematically to the *original* standard that supplies the changes. As is usually the case with thematic reference, it may or may not be intentional. When it is intentional, the soloist not only knows and has in mind some particular head, but also expects the audience to recognize it, and, if so, respond with laughter or applause.

In "Koko," as was discovered, distinct references to the original standard, "Cherokee," could be found, although Parker had been developing the main thematic focus of his solo for many years.[142] In this case, it would not have been surprising for the original material to have been entirely superseded, although traces, albeit distant ones, were present.[143] More generally, in the case of solos on changes derived from preexisting standards, it is quite possible that references to the *original* standard may be retained in the improvisation, whatever head is actually played; whether such references occur or not will depend on the standard itself and the circumstances of performance. With improvisation on rewritten rhythm-changes heads, for example, it would seem unlikely, most of the time, that references to the original "I Got Rhythm" would be heard in improvised solos, since rhythm changes as an improvisational format is so generic. This was certainly the situation in Ch. 3, for instance, in which none of the solos presented material reminiscent rhythmically or melodically of "I Got Rhythm."

When there is no theme, either stated or implied, the solo, of course, must be self-contained thematically; all coherence must be internal. The performance of "Parker's Mood," as was shown, is an intermediate instance between extremes: an introductory figure provides a source of reference and rounds out the performance, but does not substitute fully for a 12-bar theme with its potentially more elaborate thematic implications.

Formula and Its Ramifications

Thematic Reference

That formulas pervade Charlie Parker's uptempo improvisations has been demonstrated by the preceding analyses and previous studies, particularly those of Owens and Koch. The attitude and approach jazz soloists reveal towards formula are critical clues to understanding their styles. Without question, Parker's identity is strongly established by his well-known formulas, and their repeated, often predictable recurrence in similar formal and harmonic contexts.[144]

Certain formulas can be traced from soloist to soloist and effectively position the player within substyles and genres of the jazz tradition. That is, by absorbing the techniques of admired and more established improvisers through imitation of their work, jazz soloists connect to a broadly-based tradition in which material is "handed down" from player to player. It is in this sense that a player's formulas are a library created as an artistic statement, a personal signature, within a chosen stylistic tradition. Other soloists' material from the same or related traditions may be copied at first, then transformed and internalized.[145] As a result, improvisers are often recognized not only by their sound (in the most general sense: phrasing, articulation, tone, etc.), but also by the formulas they play.

Formulas can be divided into two types, small- and large-scale, which might be called, respectively, "pathways"[146] and "licks." Pathways, the shorter of the two, provide players with a working vocabulary, and in so doing facilitate performance. All improvisers, therefore, must rely on pathways in order to play freely, without undue hesitation. Developed both consciously and unconsciously, pathways "feel right" and are bound by the technical nature of the instrument itself, which determines a range of possibilities, from the available to the convenient.[147]

Sudnow (1978) demonstrates in considerable detail that a jazz soloist must develop pathways to negotiate the customary forms and harmonies found in a chosen performance style. For the pathways to be reliable, the player must be thoroughly familiar with them, even make them automatic. Although developing the pathways may be laborious at first, the player must acquire, eventually, a tactile instinct for their use: the hand must learn where to go. As the player becomes fluent in the chosen vocabulary, self-expression becomes spontaneous: the pathways become instinctive. As in speaking or typing, such fluency can only result when the operation's details are taken mostly for granted; hence internalized pathways are necessary for competent improvisational playing. In the real-time world of the improviser, spontaneity and virtuosity at bright tempos require having a lot of notes to play readily *at hand*.

More elaborately composed or patterned formulas are sometimes called "licks." Their insertion into a solo is obviously intentional, and runs the risk of sounding contrived. Practiced and eventually internalized—though not quite to the same degree as pathways—licks sometimes furnish improvisational ideas, and are always available when inspiration falters. A perhaps infamous use of licks is to provide virtuoso effects. Their overuse can lead to sterility: improvising players must constantly revise, expand, or otherwise update their licks so as to keep them sharp, if for no other reason than to avoid boredom and provide fresh contexts for their use. Ways in which this is done often include studying with other players, transcribing and learning new tunes and solos, listening to other soloists, practicing from exercise books, or studying new chord patterns and voicings. The new material so acquired may include pathways or licks, with licks being the more conscious patterns and pathways better described as "new ways of moving around."

Since all fluent improvisers must develop pathways, much jazz improvisation (uptempo, anyway) can be reduced to formula. In this sense, all competent improvisation is "formulaic"—necessarily. Hence in many of Parker's uptempo solos, virtually everything he plays is formulaic, although it is more accurate, and surely less pejorative, to conceptualize pervasive, small-scale formulas as pathways. The ingenuity disclosed in connecting pathways to more consciously developed improvisational ideas figures decisively in evaluating a player's overall skill.

The comparison of pathways to a spoken (oral) vocabulary is apt, for they consist of a small, select group of "words," readily available, and for which the speaker typically need not grope: the expression is spontaneous, the word-choice largely unplanned. Further, it is well known that speakers' oral vocabularies tend to be considerably smaller than their written ones, in which there is more time to plan word choice selectively. Perhaps because of just this time available for thought and editing, a larger vocabulary is *assumed* for written expression. Hence, verbal and literate expression are two different skills, though intimately related, since both use as their basis the vocabulary of a given language. Masters of one may not be especially skilled at the other, though each competence can and does influence the other.[148] Hence, just as readily available words and simple expressions are necessary for speech, so are pathways essential for improvisation. This, again, is why improvisation, trivially, is "formulaic."

However, not all soloists are equally dependent on licks: the number of studied phrases, consciously inserted, will vary from player to player, and indeed for a given player, from solo to solo. The interlock of pathways and licks is a function of the player's skill and general fluency.

Rather than view all improvisation as formulaic, it is more constructive
to view pathways as a necessary tool for improvisation, a large vocabulary of small "words" and short phrases that all players must develop.
Some players will rely more heavily on licks as a general feature of their
style, though, as with any such distinction, many gray areas remain.

Parker's work is not in any way compromised because he interpolated
a fairly large number of studied phrases into his uptempo improvisations.
For, as has been shown, it is not the use of practiced phrases that determines the quality of the solo, but their logic and interaction, both internally and externally, with the original thematic material. In other words,
what keeps Parker's formulas, even at the large-scale, from sounding
mechanical or stale is his ability to integrate them into a coherent whole
characterized by voice-leading fluency and subtle thematic interconnection, both internally and with the original melody. Indeed, thematic reference to the head is a dimension to Parker's playing that frequently
accompanies his best work. Sometimes conscious, sometimes unconscious, thematic references further enhance solos that are already consistent internally and may include a fairly large number of licks.

As an explanation of how unconscious thematic reference came about
in Parker's playing, the following scenario seems likely: Parker's licks
and smaller-scale formulas were combined with thematic patterns from
the head. Specifically, the original melody's thematic patterns were ap-
propriated, perhaps unwittingly, by Parker for improvisational use—the
head's "sound" and "feel" absorbed, apparently, into the solo. These
"thematic pathways," based on material from the head, were then integrated with Parker's *own* set of pathways and licks to create the solo,
which as a result acquired specific identity. The solo thereby became dif-
ferentiated from solos with similar formulas on the same changes, but
otherwise distinct thematic material.

Duplications of thematic pattern between head and solo might be hy-
pothesized to occur as a rule with good jazz players—perhaps it is even
a factor underlying the distinction between competent and outstanding
improvisation. The potential for pattern duplication also suggests why
Parker preferred to solo just after finishing the head: he may have wished
to exploit the aural and tactile qualities of the melody recently concluded; that is, while the head's sound and touch were still fresh, the solo
could be related to it more compellingly.

Of course, despite the frequency with which Parker connects to the
head via subtle thematic pathways, he sometimes refers to it clearly and
directly as well. Reasonable guesses can be made as to whether a given

reference is conscious or not, but, as argued in Ch. 2, the result is not particularly relevant to the quality of the solo or the credibility of the relationship. In all likelihood, however, Parker's more subtle references are mostly unconscious. Alternatively, when the reference *is* direct, it is probably conscious, and of course still further linkage to the original melody occurs.

Frequently, within the same solo, Parker may mix direct references to the head with more subtle thematic improvisation—as, for example in "Embraceable You" (Ch. 4). Such "in and out" reference to the head is a dual strategy that combines freer improvisation—and its more abstract thematic quality—with forthright paraphrase. It is particularly well-suited to playing ballads, where unexpected reappearances of the original melody can effectively contrast otherwise complex diminutions.

Continual and direct thematic reference, the extreme case, *is* paraphrase and provides the most straightforward method of connection to the original tune available to the soloist. Paraphrase choruses are better conceptualized as interpretations than as improvisations simply because they are intended to present the song *as* a song; improvisation, alternatively, is real-time composition. Paraphrase choruses can be brilliantly conceived, but are distinct from improvisation.

Conscious thematic reference within improvisation, as distinguished from paraphrase, is rather akin to thematic development: the solo refers to the theme concretely and at the same time is offered as original. While conscious thematic reference is certainly common in improvisation, it is possible that the more profound relationships are the more unconscious. And while it is impossible to know what Parker did or did not intend, it seems reasonable to conclude that many if not most of the subtler relationships cited in the preceding analyses were unintentional. By contrast, the direct references to the head were obvious, and sometimes, perhaps, a little disappointing: when compared to the more abstract connections, they were virtually parenthetical to the musically more compelling argument underlying the melodic surface.

Further insight on the relationship of conscious to unconscious improvisational processes can be gained from examining multiple takes in recording. In attempting to improve a solo on a given tune, Parker may or may not have had conscious alternatives or corrections in mind; sometimes, he may have merely wanted to "try another one" (play a better solo), as is often the case in jazz recording. And, whether or not he *was* conscious of take-to-take improvements, the later takes are usually the better,[149] the more convincing: it was *as if* Parker were attempting to achieve more fully, more richly, the (unconscious) artistic design of the earlier, less successful takes. For this reason—when multiple takes on a given tune were examined—it was sometimes suggested that Parker was trying to correct a "sense" of background incompleteness, or was "aiming intuitively" at a more successful integration of melody and solo, or a more coherent structural line. Single-take recordings, on the other hand, often feature an uncanny rightness—there quite simply seems to be no reason to play it again. Such instances provide further support for the suggestion that the deeper relationships in improvisation are the more unconscious.

It must be emphasized again that take-to-take improvements do not necessarily result from increased thematic relationship to the head, whether intentional or not. As was pointed out in the discussion of "Red Cross" (Ch. 3), the better of the two takes was the more indirect. Indeed, intentional thematic reference may even detract from the quality of a solo,[150] for it may be too blatant, and thereby deflect consideration of the solo's more deeply expressive properties. These more subtle underlying elements may or may not be derived from the head, but direct thematic reference can certainly overwhelm their general elusiveness. It is tempting to suggest that great structural depth and emotional range in improvisation are more likely to arise from working with familiar material ("formulas") as part of a stylistic tradition than from *intentionally* developing or referring to motives from the head.

That Parker was not especially interested in thematic *development,* despite frequent *reference* to the thematic material, reveals a key aspect of his artistry. Thematic reference differs critically from thematic development, which involves conscious and methodical repetitions, manipulations, and recombinations of the original material. For Parker, and other such soloists of his temperament, developing material in such a manner would be (1) stylistically uncharacteristic, (2) perhaps uninteresting: the soloist may not find the theme's more prominent motives particularly attractive,[151] or (3) difficult to manage in the brief time available on the three-minute, 78-rpm record.[152]

In fact, significant inclusion of large-scale formula, as frequently heard in Parker's solos, is generally incompatible with thematic development, but not thematic reference: for, if large-scale formulas extend through a solo, it is difficult to imagine how the original material could be developed simultaneously, since the inclusion of those formulas would disrupt the *process* of developing that original material—and "development" requires, conceptually, a conscious application of process.

In the more typical instance of thematic references as occurring in Parker's improvisations, their validity and cogency are not diminished merely because they occur in the context of pervasive formula.

Parallels in Oral-Epic Poetry

Formula as a key factor in improvisation and its bearing on thematic relationships recall two long-standing controversies in the study of oral-epic poetry. The parallels, indeed, are striking, and have been pointed out by other jazz analysts[153] attempting to elucidate the nature of improvisation. A glance at these issues will be helpful in placing formula in jazz improvisation in a wider context, especially as it relates to Parker and his position in Western music.

The first—and for our purposes the more relevant—issue concerns the extent to which oral poetry relies on formulas. This controversy, as we have seen with Parker, impinges closely on the definition of a formula. Lord, building on earlier work of Milman Parry, claims that in Homer formulas are "all pervasive."[154] In discussing Yugoslavian oral poetry to elucidate Homer's method, Lord writes that "there is nothing in the poem that is not formulaic."[155] Taplin describes this "building block" approach to formula as " . . . rather like a system of chemical elements which can combine in all sorts of different ways to make up different molecules."[156] As has been shown, the same can be claimed of Parker's improvisational method, especially in uptempo solos, many of which can be parsed into a continuous sequence of formulas.

Critics responded to the Parry-Lord approach by pointing out that the subtlety and depth of great oral poetry—Homer's work in particular—go beyond the mechanical quality implied by the formula concept.[157] Taplin, for example, warns that "There has been a tendency, however—partly due perhaps to the molecular or 'building block' analogy—to reckon the range of combinations and possibilities of expression to be far more limited than they are."[158]

Thus, analysis by formula citation in oral poetry has proven just as problematic as it has in jazz: while the practice needs to be taken into account, overemphasis on formula overlooks much of the expressivity, the "music," of the artwork. Part of the problem, as pointed out by Finnegan,[159] is that a too-inclusive view of formula seems to encompass virtually anything played. In addition, it should be noted that through such analysis the artwork is seen *as* a mix of formulas—as a kind of robotic insertion of cliché into some convenient niche—rather than as expressive, living, composition. Thus, in the analysis of oral poetry, as in jazz, emphasis on the formulaic aspects of the artwork has been seen as denigrating the artwork.

A part of the problem, as suggested in the previous section, might be an unfortunate word choice. "Formulaic" connotes "mechanical," "formula," "cliché." But the use of formula, in either jazz or oral poetry, as has been shown, is surely not mechanical when the best artworks are involved. A more constructive ambience for analytical discussion follows when "formulaic" is avoided; analysis can proceed by citing formulas where relevant to the argument, but the work or passages of it should not be described simply as "formulaic," followed by a listing of the formulas. Such a procedure does not do justice to the artwork by any measure.

The second of the controversies in oral poetry is the extent to which writing was adopted as an aid to composition.[160] This issue ultimately impinges on Parker's improvisational methods, his compositions, and, more broadly, on the nature of jazz as an art form within the context of Western cultural history.

After considerable disagreement and discussion, it currently seems the dominant, perhaps even the established,[161] view that much of Homer's poetry was composed with the aid of writing, but that formula-based passages can be found in the work's final form because of its genesis in the oral tradition.[162] The issues here are technical, and, given the age of and lack of information on the poetry involved, probably will continue to remain controversial. Nevertheless, there is reason to conclude that the finest oral poetry, as in Homer's work, is much too subtly constructed, on both the small- and large-scale, to have been totally improvised. In all likelihood, orally produced sections were compiled and refined by a single poet (Homer?) with literate assistants, or perhaps by a small group of poets who may have revised and reworked previous versions of the work.

Literacy and its Role in the Jazz Tradition

In this section and the next, the role of literacy in the jazz tradition will be explored, in order to help place Parker's contributions—and that of bop more generally—in the context of Western musical history. This very general discussion of recent trends in both popular and fine-art music hypothesizes, particularly, that the oral element of jazz culture and the acquistion of fine-art status of some jazz substyles since the bop era have accelerated the acceptance and development of formula-based music since the mid-20th century. The extent to which Parker, perhaps unsurpassed as jazz performer and stylistic innovator, exemplifies both bop and the idea of the orally-based musician as fine artist is another measure of his historical significance.

If the description of the genesis of the Homeric epics in the previous section is valid, jazz correlates readily come to mind: some big bands in the 1920s and 1930s, for example, occasionally developed material through communal head arrangements (the oral tradition), which afterwards might be shaped by an arranger into a more finished product (the literate). Larger-scale jazz compositions are perhaps another step in the direction of the literate. For example, some works, normally thought as part of the jazz oeuvre, are almost entirely written, for example, Ellington's,[163] or Gil Evans's. Groups and artists working in "free jazz" genres will tend to emphasize the oral: ironically, despite the aesthetic difficulty and fine-art intentions of their music, they connect more directly to folk traditions based on oral culture—an important stylistic antecedent of jazz—than do groups relying on a more "arranged" sound or on the popular-song tradition.

As noted earlier in this chapter, Parker was a literate musician—at least to the extent of being able to read music—but was not especially committed to developing his art as composition and arrangement through the written tradition. While he surely could write lead sheets and was able to function as a section player in big bands, he was evidently more concerned with music as oral expression. For Parker to have involved himself in more experimental or large-scale composition would have necessitated a fundamental change of musical attitude—and such a step he never took: once musicians abandon composing as providing material for improvisation, their writing tends to gravitate toward the ambience of the art-music tradition, where a more detailed knowledge of form, of methods of development, harmony, counterpoint, and orchestration, involve extended study. Parker, by remaining in song-based formats that could be mastered orally, avoided such extensions, although his reported interest in twentieth century art music shows a desire for experimentation that for various reasons was never pursued.

Yet while Parker remained a more oral than literate musician, he was certainly literate, at least minimally. Such a background in both the oral and written is typical of improvising jazz players. Melodic formulas, concepts of tone and phrasing, and even harmonic principles may be acquired from more established and admired players through the oral tradition, yet many (if not most) players have also relied on written music as an aid to development: studying pedagogical exercises, transcribing passages too difficult to learn by ear, or memorizing solos transcribed by others, for example.

While it has long been thought that these are modern developments, that the earlier players who innovated jazz as a distinct musical style were probably orally-based musicians, jazz has always involved written work. Indeed, the relationship between the oral and written in early jazz remains controversial. Witness the importance of lead sheets, written arrangements, the genesis of some early groups in New Orleans brass bands, or the importance of classically trained Creole musicians to the founding of early jazz. While the role of the solo improviser might, at first glance, seem anchored in the oral tradition, this was a relatively late development in jazz history, occurring in the 1920s. In the formative history of jazz, from, say 1910–1920, group playing, sometimes based on written arrangements, was the norm.

The mixture of the oral and written traditions has been one of the prime factors in the establishment of the numerous jazz substyles and crossover hybrids; in this respect, the mixture of the oral and written has added to the notorious difficulty of finding a widely acceptable definition of "jazz." Certain purists insist that for music to be jazz, it must be (mostly) improvised. This definition of jazz is probably too narrow and may be based on a view of the music formed during the emergence in the 1920s of the featured soloist—when improvisation, now taken to be the essence of jazz, was assumed to be also the essence of its prehistory. Definitions of "jazz" that attempt to be comprehensive will probably be *too* inclusive, but this seems more fruitful than trying to delimit such a wideranging and richly multiform art by identifying it exclusively with the improvised solo and its basis in oral culture.

Despite the complex overlap of the oral and the literate that characterizes jazz, it has rightly been considered an orally-*based* art form; and it is in view of this consideration that the evolution of jazz at least does redress a certain balance in Western art music, which, in uninterrupted evolution from the Middle Ages, had been in danger of drifting too far afield from *its* basis in the oral tradition. For by the early twentieth century, only oral vestiges in concert music would remain—it had become an entirely literate art form for all intents and purposes, as spontaneous composition and expression came to be discouraged. Concert-music pedagogy in our time has continued to emphasize skillful (if not artistic) rendering of written music to the exclusion of the improvised—not only by performers, but even by those wishing to become composers. The division itself between players and composers has become sacrosanct during the twentieth century, though this has not generally been true through much of Western music history.

In jazz, alternatively, improvising, orally-based players, commonly compose and view the activity as normal, as a natural function of being musical. The major departure from the oral for such musicians, as mentioned above, is the decision to approach composition as something other than providing new heads for improvisation. The extent to which such a larger-scale approach is adopted will align the musician to a greater or lesser extent with the concert tradition and the training required for producing compositions and arrangements. But jazz musicians, typified by Parker, generally proceed from an oral, improvisatory basis as the foundation of their art, despite personal differences and mixtures of the oral and literate. Thus it is possible that jazz in the totality of its numerous genres, which run the gamut from popular to fine-art culture, marks a very large-scale return of Western art music to its oral roots. This return was precipitated early in the century by a new musical style and outlook, soon to be called "jazz," and formed from a mixture of the European tradition with a renewed emphasis on oral culture whose roots reached back to Africa.

Large-Scale Impact on Contemporary Music

In the late twentieth century, formulas, both melodic and rhythmic, pervade much contemporary music, influencing styles from jazz, through popular genres, over to concert formats. This situation is radically different from, say, the status of popular and fine-art music in the West a century ago—before the broad influence of jazz and other African-American styles on our musical culture. The type of formula heard in contemporary music differs according to the musical context: for example, jazz-based styles might feature improvisatory formulas not unlike Parker's; in concert styles, the application might be more literally repetitive; in popular styles, melodic fragments might be digitally sampled and looped. In all these styles, but especially in popular and jazz-rock contexts, background textures may be constructed from combining rhythmic and melodic formulas from different instruments or electronic sound sources.

The type of formula heard in improvisation, and typified by Parker in bop, prefigured and in part set the stage culturally for the current vogue of formula-based styles: for while Parker's style is certainly a product of the jazz tradition and could not be confused with the formula-based

textures heard in some contemporary nonjazz styles, it seems possible
that Parker's brilliance and pursuance of jazz as an art form have created
an atmosphere in which formula-based music could not only be ac-
cepted, but also thrive. Parker is not directly responsible for this development, of course; but he is perhaps the prime exemplar of the fine-art
tradition in jazz, as first manifested in bebop.

Many contemporary styles develop formulas through intense repetition, gradual evolution, and, as a result, present a rather strictly unfolding temporal space, all of which combine to engage the listener on a more
broadly visceral level than is possible with more tightly developed, non-
repetitive musical forms. Popular styles may rely on strophic repetition
in the form of vamps, and in so doing extend and connect to the song tradition, whereas concert contexts will tend to be more open-ended formally. Jazz, depending on the substyle, may or may not be structured
by strophic repetition. In all of these styles, though, the danger of over-
reliance on repetitive textures is a certain "thinness," or lack of traditional musical interest, which can render repeated performances flat. The
balance between a more formula-based and a more thematically non-
repetitive quality to the music depends on the style of the performer, or
composer, and the function and intent of the music itself.

Pervasive application of formula is particularly appropriate in certain
jazz and popular styles, not surprisingly, given their closer association
with the oral tradition. The effect of these styles derives from the African
side of the jazz tradition and popular music with African-American
roots. In more popular styles, it is associated with the hypnotic quality of
the "groove" produced by an effective rhythm section or the interlock of
rhythmically-based parts, as in synthesizer sequencing; in jazz, groove
is often present as well—particularly in jazz-rock or funk-based styles.
In a more mainstream style (and sometimes free jazz), a sense of groove
is associated with formula-based improvisation as a conscious, "ex-
ploratory," tool—as, preeminently, in the work of John Coltrane. It is in
such jazz applications that the immediate legacy of Parker's work is most
evident. What makes a groove "good" is rather akin to what makes more
traditional jazz "swing."[164]

While late nineteenth-century concert music avoided consistent application of formula, such styles are common enough now to merit a
generic name: "process music," with Philip Glass its most well known
composer. It is perhaps not coincidental that *the* ground-breaking concert work of the century—were a single work to be selected—is Stravinsky's *Le Sacre du Printemps*, which emphasizes percussion and juxta-

poses formulaic rhythmic patterns with hitherto unheard-of intensity. In the concert world, this work helped set the stage for the more modern and consistent formula application, as well as the focus on percussion. Stravinsky continued extensive use of formula within the context of ritual in such follow-up works as *Les Noces*. Despite his evolution into a more neoClassic style in the 1920s and thereafter, aspects of formula persist throughout his oeuvre.

The persistent application of formula also creates a sense of ritual, which in both fine-art and more popular styles, has become more important to Western musical culture in the late twentieth century.[165] The incantatory aesthetic of groove and ritual, so characteristic of the music in our time, is culturally revolutionary when viewed on the large scale: it can be argued, for example, that it reverses a dominant trend in Western art music from the Middle Ages to mid-twentieth century modernism, which, in its major statements, such as the sonata-allegro movement, viewed small-scale repetition circumspectly. With the obvious exceptions of theme and variations models and more popularly-based material, works of major import and length were created through increased complexity, not formula or strophic repetition. This idea is a major principle behind the Schenkerian *Ursatz*, which might underlie the 8-bar melody, and on a vaster (and far less determinate) scale, the 500-bar sonata-allegro movement.

In the twentieth century, Schoenberg avoided exact repetition in following the lead established by various Romantic composers—particularly Wagner and Mahler—but was troubled by the difficulties of creating music without simple repetition, an attribute characteristic of his style and modernism generally. Indeed, he developed the 12-tone method in order to create the potential of large-scale formal relationships in lieu of the hierarchical nesting provided systemically by tonality. The legacy of Schoenberg among composers who cite him as a stylistic antecedent continues through their avoidance of obvious repetition. Such post-Schoenberg styles are cultural counterbalances to the formula-based approaches heard in process music. Each tendency emphasizes, perhaps to an extreme, repetition or nonrepetition—and can be defined therefore in relation to formula use or avoidance.

It is curious that the traditional qualities of Western fine-art music, such as conciseness and thematic interrelationship, may be effective within music that is groove-based, but that crossover musics are perhaps less successful in concert surroundings. As is evident in classical programs attempting to project an authentic jazz ambience, orchestras are not known for their swing or groove in the African-American tradition. This may be because interaction between the written and the oral has always been part of the jazz tradition, whereas concert music in recent centuries has distanced itself too far from the oral to be entirely comfortable in its presence. Concert performers, as a result, lack training in projecting the essence of an orally-based style; and the conductor occasionally seems superfluous. Additionally, ritualistic music is usually percussion-based and involves repetitive time-keeping, neither of which is associated with traditional fine-art ensembles and their string-based textures. On the other hand, this century's radical increase in the use of percussion underlies the distinction between the sound of the classical and modern orchestra, and helps make the modern ensemble compatible with more formula-based music. Thus, contemporary developments are providing bridges between formula-based and more traditionally conceived styles, so that, in the concert tradition anyway, the distinction may not obtain much longer. A more likely distinction that will continue is that which distinguishes fine-art and more popular genres: structural complexity and depth of expression. This distinction should remain, therefore, largely intact, despite postmodern attempts to merge the two.

Further discussion of the many topics that arise from the embrace or avoidance of formula-based styles, in both jazz and concert music, remain outside the scope of this study. It is more relevant to my purpose here, in discussing Charlie Parker's music, to hint at the importance of these issues in order to show that the renewed emphasis on oral expression and formula, as typified in his work and bop more generally, have provided the West in this century with new possibilities for growth, not only within jazz but also within the totality of musical culture.

Parker's Balance of Formula and
Traditional Western Values

It remains for us — in conclusion — to show how these more broadly cultural issues affect an assessment of Parker's position within jazz history. We should begin by noting that Parker, despite his closeness to and affinity with the folk origins of jazz, was not a ritualistic player, even in his multi-chorus, more informally recorded solos (with possible exceptions in his blues playing, to be noted below). The more ritualistic application of improvisatory formula in jazz achieves a certain apotheosis in the later work of John Coltrane. Continuing legacies include the many jazz performers who acknowledge Coltrane as a principal stylistic predecessor and influence. By contrast, Parker's formulas are heard within an unprecedentedly flexible and virtuosic improvised line closely associated with the more traditional Western values of harmony and voice leading.

The application of formula in bebop thus antedates its use in many contemporary jazz and non-jazz styles where intensity, repetition, and through-composed form are paramount. As groove requires more than three minutes for the creation of a ritualistic ambience, so it was less common in Parker's day when jazz was associated more with a song-based popular culture and recording time was limited. Nor is a modern sense of groove conspicuous in longer, more informally recorded jam sessions or live performances. Perhaps it is mostly closely approximated by the emphasis on riff heard in the blues and blues-affected styles of Kansas City (Basie, McShann and the like), as captured in informal jam sessions, or in extended performances such as the "Jazz at the Philharmonic" concerts. It is to this extent and in such contexts that Parker's work occasionally tilts toward the modern. But Parker's style is still based on formula: as noted above, its influence and the establishment of jazz as an art form may have helped provide a cultural atmosphere in which contemporary styles, relying ever more extensively on formula, could achieve acceptance.

It was noted in the previous section that while distinctions are currently being eroded between various musical styles, the fine-art, popular-art gamut is likely to remain valid, since it is based on the complexity, function, and expressive intent of the works produced.[166] The structural richness and expressive depth of Parker's work position him as a bridge between the fine-art and the popular, with an unmistakable emphasis towards the fine-art side of the cultural spectrum. As bop style's premier musician, Parker was perhaps the most influential exponent in the large-scale redefinition of jazz, since the mid-1940s, as an art form. Parker's relationship to the high- and popular-art worlds thus parallels the status of jazz itself in contemporary culture — and strengthens Parker's stature as one of the two or three most influential jazz musicians of all time, and perhaps its greatest improviser.

Parker's best work is fitted ideally to the three-minute medium, his one or two choruses not unlike the understated perfection of a Chopin Waltz, Debussy or Bach Prelude, or Schubert Impromptu. It is here that Parker creates his most memorable (though perhaps not his most adventurous) work: for within the one- or two-chorus form, Parker must unfold his best material as quickly as possible. Without the luxury of

stretching out, the heart of his musical conception must be presented suc-
cinctly. In those live recordings where Parker indulges in extended and
experimental solos, his work is exciting and sometimes exhilarating, but
not as fully satisfying as his shorter work, as typified by the studio
recordings. It is in the three-minute medium that Parker, in his best performances, ideally combines the use of formula as a necessary part
of improvisation with the perfected, no-loose-ends economy of well-
crafted composition in the tonal tradition.

Thus Parker's finest improvisations are gem-like miniatures, expres-
sively rooted in oral culture, yet exemplifying, on a small scale, the sub-
tlest fine-art desiderata. These solos are prime examples of "musical
maximalism"—the most that *can* be done in the shortest time. In a masterful Parker solo, every note works, no detail is ignored, every moment
counts. At the same time, Parker's solos may allude directly to the motives of the head, sometimes in paraphrase, or to its more abstract structural features—and in so doing transcend characterization as a sequence
of motivic formulas. Indeed, Parker ingeniously projected the melodies
he played, whether written extemporaneously for the session or widely
familiar as standards. Parker may have internalized not only the aural
qualities of the head, but also its fingering—its actual feel. The resulting
thematic connections were deep, sometimes hidden, and almost definitely unconscious. It is through these uncommonly subtle transforma-
tions of the original thematic material that Charlie Parker's improvisations achieve their highest levels.

Works Cited

Bibliography

Boardman, John, Jasper Griffin and Oswyn Murray. 1986. *The Oxford History of the Classical World*. Oxford and New York: Oxford University Press.

Cadwallader, Allen and William Pastille. 1992. "Schenker's High-Level Motives." *Journal of Music Theory* 36/1 (Spring, 1992): 119–48.

Cooper, Grosvenor and Leonard B. Meyer. 1960. *The Rhythmic Structure of Music*. Chicago and London: The University of Chicago Press.

Finnegan, Ruth. 1977. *Oral Poetry: Its Nature, Significance and Social Context*. Cambridge: Cambridge University Press.

Gennari, John. 1991. "Jazz Criticism: Its Development and Ideologies." *Black American Literature Forum* 25/3 (Fall, 1991): 449–523.

Giddins, Gary. 1981. *Riding on a Blue Note: Jazz and American Pop*. New York and Oxford: Oxford University Press.

Gushee, Lawrence. 1981. "Lester Young's 'Shoeshine Boy.'" *Report of the Twelfth Congress, Berkeley, 1977*. Kassel: International Musicological Society. Reprint in Porter 1991.

Harrison, Max. 1976. *A Jazz Retrospect*. New York: Crescendo Publishing.

———. 1959. "Charlie Parker." in Hentoff and McCarthy 1959.

Hentoff, Nat and Nat Shapiro. 1955. *Hear Me Talkin' to Ya*. New York: Rinehart and Company, Inc. Reprint, New York: Dover Publications, 1966.

Hentoff, Nat and Albert J. McCarthy. 1959. *Jazz*. New York: Rinehart and Company, Inc. Reprint, New York: Da Capo, 1975.

Hodeir, André. 1956. *Jazz, Its Evolution and Essence*. New York: Grove Press.

Jaffe, Andrew. 1983. *Jazz Theory*. Dubuque, Iowa: William C. Brown Company.

Jeppesen, Knud. [1946] 1970. *The Style of Palestrina and the Dissonance*. New York: Dover Publications. [Original publ. by Oxford University Press.]

Kalib, Sylvan Sol. 1973. "Thirteen Essays from the Three Yearbooks *Das Meisterwerk in der Musik* by Heinrich Schenker: An Annotated Translation." Ph.D. diss., Northwestern University.

Kernfeld, Barry. 1988. "Improvisation." *New Grove Dictionary of Jazz*, vol. 2, 554–63. London and New York: Macmillan.

———. 1983. "Two Coltranes." *Annual Review of Jazz Studies* 2: 7–66.

Koch, Lawrence O. 1974, 1975a. "Ornithology: A Study of Charlie Parker's

Music." *Journal of Jazz Studies*, 2/1 (Dec., 1974): 61–87 and 2/2 (June, 1975): 61–85.

————. 1975b. "A Numerical Listing of Charlie Parker's Recordings." *Journal of Jazz Studies* 2/2 (June, 1975): 86–95.

————. 1988. *Yardbird Suite: A Compendium of the Music and Life of Charlie Parker.* Bowling Green, Ohio: Bowling Green State University Popular Press.

Lerdahl, Fred and Ray Jackendoff. 1983. *A Generative Theory of Tonal Music.* Cambridge, Mass: The MIT Press.

Levin, Michael and John S. Wilson. [1949] 1994. "No Bop Roots in Jazz: Parker." *Down Beat* 61/2 (Feb., 1994), 24–6.

Levine, Mark. 1989. *The Jazz Piano Book.* Petaluma, California: Sher Music Co.

Lloyd-Jones, Hugh. 1992. "Becoming Homer." *New York Review of Books* 36/5 (March 5. 1992): 52–7.

Lord, Albert. 1960. *The Singer of Tales.* Cambridge, Mass: Harvard University Press.

Martin, Henry. 1988. "Jazz Harmony: A Syntactic Background." *Annual Review of Jazz Studies 4* : 9–30.

Meyer, Leonard B. 1973. *Explaining Music.* Chicago and London: University of Chicago Press.

Narmour, Eugene. 1977. *Beyond Schenkerism: The Need for Alternatives in Music Analysis.* Chicago and London: University of Chicago Press.

Owens, Thomas. 1974. "Charlie Parker: Techniques of Improvisation." Ph.D. diss., University of California-Los Angeles.

Patrick, James. 1988. "Charlie Parker," *New Grove Dictionary of Jazz,* vol. 2, 286–91. London and New York: Macmillan.

————. 1975. "Charlie Parker and Harmonic Sources of Bebop Composition." *Journal of Jazz Studies* 2/2 (June, 1975): 3–23.

————. 1978. "Notes." *Charlie Parker—The Complete Savoy Studio Sessions.* New York: Savoy CD ZDS-5500.

————. 1990. "Notes." *The Complete Dean Benedetti Recordings of Charlie Parker.* Stamford, Conn.: Mosaic CD MD7-129.

Porter, Lewis, Michael Ullman and Ed Hazell. 1993. *Jazz: From Its Origins to the Present.* Englewood Cliffs, New Jersey: Prentice Hall.

Porter, Lewis, ed. 1991. *A Lester Young Reader.* Washington and London: The Smithsonian Institution Press.

Rink, John. 1993. "Schenker and Improvisation." *Journal of Music Theory* 37/1 (Spring 1993): 1–54.

Saks, Norman, Leonard Bukowski, and Robert M. Bregman. 1989. *Yardbird Inc—The Charlie Parker Discography.* 54 Rockledge Path, Port Jefferson, NY 11177: BBS.

Schenker, Heinrich. [1925] 1973. "The Art of Improvisation." Trans. Sylvan Kalib. "Thirteen Essays from the Three Yearbooks *Das Meisterwerk in der*

Musik by Heinrich Schenker: An Annotated Translation." Ph.D. diss., Northwestern University,

————. [1910, 1922] 1987. *Counterpoint*. 2 vols. Trans. John Rothgeb and Jürgen Thym; ed. John Rothgeb. New York: Schirmer Books.

————. [1935] 1979. *Free Composition*. Trans. and ed. Ernst Oster. New York: Schirmer Books.

Schuller, Gunther. 1958. "Sonny Rollins and the Challenge of Thematic Improvisation," *The Jazz Review* 1 (Nov., 1958). Reprinted in *Musings—The Musical Worlds of Gunther Schuller*. New York and Oxford: Oxford University Press, 1986.

Shive, David M. 1987. *Naming Achilles*. Oxford and New York: Oxford University Press.

Smith, Gregory. 1983. "Homer, Gregory, and Bill Evans? The Theory of Formulaic Composition in the Context of Jazz Piano Improvisation." Ph. D. diss., Harvard University.

Stewart, Milton L. 1974–5. "Structural Development in the Jazz Improvisational Technique of Clifford Brown." *Jazz Forschung (Jazz Research)* 6/7: 141–273.

Strunk, Steven. 1985. "Bebop Melodic Lines: Tonal Characteristics." *Annual Review of Jazz Studies* 3: 97–120.

————. 1979. "The Harmony of Early Bop: A Layered Approach." *Journal of Jazz Studies* 6/1 (Fall/Winter, 1979): 4–53.

Sudnow, David. 1978. *Ways of the Hand: The Organization of Improvised Conduct*. New York: Harper Colophon (Harper and Row).

Taplin, Oliver. 1986. "Homer." *The Oxford History of the Classical World*. Oxford and New York: Oxford University Press.

Tirro, Frank. 1977. *Jazz, A History*. New York: Norton.

————. 1967. "The Silent Theme Tradition in Jazz." *The Musical Quarterly* 53/3 (July, 1967): 313–334.

Williams, J. Kent. 1988. "Archetypal Schemata in Jazz Themes of the Bebop Era," *Annual Review of Jazz Studies* 4: 49–74.

Wimsatt, W. K. and Monroe Beardsley. 1946. "The Intentional Fallacy." *The Sewanee Review* 54/3: 468–88.

Discography

Ballads and Birdland. Mark Records MG 101.

The Complete Dean Benedetti Recordings of Charlie Parker. Mosaic CD MD7-129.

Bird: The Complete Charlie Parker on Verve. Verve CD 837 141–2.

Early Bird. Stash CD 542.

Quintessential Jazz at Massey Hall. Original Jazz Classics CD-OJC-044.

The Complete Dial Sessions. Stash CD ST-CD-567-68-69-70.

Bird at St. Nick's. JWS Jazz Workshop CD 500

Bebop & Bird. Hipsville/Rhino CD R2 70198.

Charlie Parker—The Complete Savoy Studio Sessions, Savoy CD ZDS-5500.

The Smithsonian Collection of Classic Jazz, Smithsonian Books and Recordings CD 2502.

Stearns, Marshall and John Maher. 1950. "Interview with Charlie Parker," probably May 1, 1950. Philology CD 57-2. Also transcribed by Mark Gardner in *Jazz Journal* 17/5 (May, 1964): 25–6.

Notes

1. Mosaic CD MD7-129.
2. Primarily Owens 1974, and Koch 1974 and 1975a. These will be cited extensively, especially Owens 1974.
3. "Tune" is in common use among jazz musicians to refer to popular standards or jazz melodies. The word is by no means pejorative. "Head" refers to whatever thematic material (usually a tune) was played as a basis for the improvisations.
4. As will become evident in the theoretical discussions of Ch. 2, my use of the term "thematic improvisation" is broadened from its prevailing use, which refers to explicit development of foreground motives. This more common understanding of the term may be traced to Schuller 1958 in his influential study of Sonny Rollins's "Blue Seven." For an overview of this topic see Kernfeld (1988, 1, 559–61). As part of the general theme of this book, I hope to show that improvisation need not be explicitly developmental in order to be considered thematic.
5. Owens 1974, 1, 269.
6. See Owens 1974, 2, 1–10. Since this list will commonly be referred to in identifying formulas, redundant references to Owens's dissertation and page number will be omitted in the notes to follow.
7. Patrick 1988, 288.
8. Harrison 1959, 282.
9. Owens 1974, 1, 269.
10. That Parker's solos are indeed intimately connected to the original melodies seems to have been suggested elliptically by André Hodeir (1956, 100), but without specific analytical verification:

   > ... Parker now and again lets the phrase-pretext [the phrase occurring at that point in the original melody] put in a brief appearance, but at other times it can only be guessed at behind the garland of notes in which it is embedded and which, far from being useless embroidery, form by themselves a perfectly articulated musical discourse of which the theme, hidden or expressed, is merely one of the constituent elements.

11. The term "rhythm changes" refers to the harmonies or chord "changes" of George and Ira Gershwin's "I Got Rhythm" (1930), although jazz musicians

normally revise its original 34-bar structure into a symmetrical, 32-bar AABA form with each section eight bars long. This layout is analyzed in the next chapter. Jazz musicians have long been fond of inserting new tunes over the harmonic structure of popular songs, both for inspirational stimulus and to avoid copyright fees. This practice has been studied by Tirro 1967, 313–34; and Patrick 1975, 3–23. In the latter article, Patrick, drawing an analogy with medieval practice, refers to the new compositions as "contrafacts" (5). More commonly, the newly written melody is called a "jazz tune" to distinguish it categorically from a popular standard. Of course, jazz tunes do not have to be based on previous material.

12. By totaling individual studio takes, private recordings (which continue to surface), and live broadcasts, the total number of Parker's recordings seems to be roughly 1400, according to Patrick (personal communication). Parker's studio recordings include 427 individual takes, however, and these would seem to be preferred for judging the relative importance of competing improvisational vehicles. Based on the studio sample, rhythm changes and blues far outdistance any other formal improvisational paradigms. The next most common consist of "How High the Moon" (8 percent) and "What Is This Thing Called Love?" (5 percent). These numbers are derived from discussion with Patrick and discographical sources such as Koch 1988 and Saks-Bukowski-Bregman 1989.

13. As can be inferred from Owens 1974, 1, *passim*, in his analyses of Parker's style according to key.

14. To clarify this tripartite categorization of Parker's work: (1) *Jazz tunes* (numerous rhythm-changes heads, for example): usually written by jazz musicians, these are entirely original or based on the harmonic structure of some pre-existing melody. Jazz musicians will tend to be familiar with this repertoire and categorize a melody as such. (2) *Popular tunes or standards:* these are more likely to be known by the general public. (3) *Blues.* Overlap of genres is common: "St. Louis Blues" (Handy) can be thought of as a popular song, for example.

15. Owens 1974, 1, 35.

16. Owens applies Schenker-like analysis to Parker's work, but his sketches are not revealing of thematic differences among the solos. Rather, Owens uses voice-leading techniques to show how *alike* Parker's solos are to one another. Consider his statement, "More examples [Schenker-like analyses of rhythm changes] from other pieces and other keys could be cited, but they would add relatively little additional information." (1974, 1, 239) In sum, Owens's use of Schenker-based techniques is rather half-hearted, as is evident where he states that applying "Salzerian [or Schenkerian] analysis [to improvisation] may seem to be stretching a point." (1974, 1, 219). He does not elaborate on how this is so. His analyses (1974, 1, 219–66) do show that Parker's large-scale forms often employ Schenkerian background forms, or their variants, and descending phrase patterns—and at one point, in an

analysis of "The Closer" (1974, 1, 221–3), Owens observes that Parker often delayed structural tones in order to create more interesting melodic approaches to them. This point, as well as Parker's use of descending passages and Schenker-like background forms, will be confirmed in the analyses to follow.

17. Other Schenker-influenced studies in jazz include Stewart 1974–75 and Smith 1983. Stewart's work is especially detailed, consisting of a large-scale analysis of a single Clifford Brown solo.

18. The "original changes" may either be notated on the published sheet music or transcribed from the first recording. And the latter harmonies may in themselves differ from what is given on the published sheet music. Further, there may even be inconsistencies on the published sheet music itself, such as the chord symbols differing from what is notated in the piano part.

19. In the well-known modification of "I Can't Get Started" by Dizzy Gillespie, the II-V chord sequence in mm. 3-4 clashes with the pick-up to m. 5. Hear The Dizzy Gillespie Sextet: "I Can't Get Started" (Duke, Gershwin), recorded January 9, 1945, for Manor (New York City). Dizzy Gillespie, trumpet; Trummy Young, trombone; Don Byas, tenor saxophone, Clyde Hart, piano; Oscar Pettiford, bass; Shelly Manne, drums. Available on The Smithsonian Collection of Recordings, CD 2502.

20. In "comping," the pianist or guitarist provides a harmonic-rhythmic accompaniment—usually with punctuated chords.

21. A basic knowledge of bop harmony—available in previous work of Strunk 1979, Martin 1988, Levine 1989, or Jaffe 1983—is assumed.

22. Strunk 1979 and Martin 1988 discuss in detail the hierarchical analysis of the large-scale harmonic structure in bop. Strunk in particular provides rules that derive bop-style progressions in the manner demonstrated in this section.

23. For details, see Martin 1988.

24. "Autumn Leaves" (Mercer, Prevert, Kosma), 1955.

25. "Sweet Georgia Brown" (Bernie, Pinkard, Casey), 1925.

26. "Jazz Me Blues" (Delaney), 1921. Analyzed in Martin 1988, 12–5.

27. Thelonious Monk's "Skippy" features experimental changes that eventually establish Ab major as a tonic by arrival. Its changes generally descend by half step or perfect fifth —and are thereby seemingly functional—but normative procedures that establish and relate tonics at the ends of regular phrases and sections are avoided.

28. Much of the voice-leading analysis in this study is based on an adaptation of Heinrich Schenker's work, as will become clear in this section. Schenker himself deals with improvisation in his essay, "The Art of Improvisation," from *Das Meisterwerk in der Musik* (Schenker [1925] 1973). Discussing C. P. E. Bach's *Versuch über die wahre Art das Clavier zu spielen [Essay on the True Art of Playing Keyboard Instruments]* as a starting point, Schenker analyzes the composition of a free fantasia and standard practices of ornamentation

rather than improvisation on a prior work or on some standard model (such as the blues), and so his essay is not directly relevant to the issues raised here. Nevertheless, in a broad sense both Schenker and C. P. E. Bach (in Schenker's citations) formulate improvisation as diminution of conceptually prior harmonies—the same process underlying jazz improvisation. See Rink 1993 for further study of Schenker's concept of improvisation. Rink, interestingly, supplies serveral quotations that suggest Schenker greatly lamented the decline of improvisation in the European fine-art tradition. I will allude to this topic again in the final chapter.

29. Schenker *Counterpoint* 1 [1910, 1922], 1987, 94–100. I apply the notion of melodic fluency to bop.

30. Martin 1988 and Strunk 1985 derive voice-leading analyses similar to those developed in this chapter.

31. Strunk 1985, 98. The article includes a useful summary of the resolving tendencies of the various tensions commonly heard in bop lines and an analysis of Parker's "Donna Lee." Voice leading is also treated, though less systematically, in Jaffe 1983, 21–43.

32. Dizzy Gillespie's All Star Quintet: "Shaw 'Nuff" (Parker, Gillespie), recorded May 11, 1945, for Guild (New York City). Charlie Parker, alto sax; Dizzy Gillespie, trumpet; Al Haig, piano; Curly Russell, bass; Sidney Catlett, drums. Available on The Smithsonian Collection of Recordings, CD 2502.

33. Viewing a single melodic line segmented into a multi-part score helps counter a standard criticism of voice-leading analysis. Opponents sometimes claim that such analysis takes the rhythm of the music insufficiently into account—that something is amiss when pitches important to the overall musical effect are depicted as unimportant or even "decorative" in the analysis. For example, a nonchord tone may be critical to the overall effect of the line, but then is rendered as a stemless notehead on a voice-leading sketch; this occurred with the B♭4's in m. 1 of the Bach *Violin Partita* (Ex. 2–5). But when this occurs in analysis—and it occurs often—an important insight is revealed: the musical effect created is a product of *just* this contrast—the "irony"—of the pitch's lesser importance to the larger-scale harmony versus its foreground prominence dynamically. Other analytical methods may approach more directly the issue of the rhythm of events in a musical work, but voice-leading analysis will still yield considerable rhythmic insight through its depiction of *how* the passage's harmonic progress is positioned against the overall rhythmic flow. An approach to analysis that is in debt to Schenker's work, but directly tackles the issue of harmonic prolongation versus an often-contrasting metrical effect, is Lerdahl-Jackendoff 1983—for example in the authors' distinction between "time-span reduction" and "prolongational reduction."

34. This issue is treated in Martin 1988, 10–12, where a circle-of-fifths pattern with seventh chords is shown to underlie much harmonic progression in the jazz styles up to and including bop.

35. Tiny Grimes Quintet: "Red Cross" (Charlie Parker), recorded for Savoy, September 15, 1944 (WOR Studios, New York City). Two takes: S5713-1 and S5713-2. Charlie Parker, alto saxophone; Clyde Hart, piano; Tiny Grimes, guitar; Jimmy Butts, bass; Harold "Doc" West, drums. Available on Savoy ZDS-5500.

36. The term "primary tone" (a translation of *Kopfton* — Schenker [1935] 1979, 38) in Ex. 2–10, is applied to the B$\hat{3}$, not because of any allegiance to Schenkerian orthodoxy, but rather that *in this case* its use seems convincing. Terms such as "fundamental lines" and *"Ursatz"* will be used similarly when they *do* seem to help convey the relationships posited by the analysis. The other options, either coining new terms or taking the terms of less familiar theories, would only serve to complicate the discussion and perhaps commit the analysis to these theories. In any event, voice-leading analysis, based on the standard resolving tendencies and innate hierarchization of bop harmony, is only one of the methods used to discuss Parker's work. Very often, my argument for the existence of thematic relationships proceeds from a variety of more general principles, as clarified below and in the next section.

37. Schenker's own thinking led him to abandon the concept of the motive entirely (See Cadwallader-Pastille 1992, 135), but this seems too radical a step. A more reasonable position, as these authors suggest, is to apply the term "motive" hierarchically.

38. See Cadwallader-Pastille 1992, 140–44.

39. But not always: consider the different harmonic functions of a tonic I chord in root position vs. a I$^6_4$ chord, for example.

40. A further complication is that the players may not always agree on the chord being played, as pointed out earlier.

41. Schenker admits this implicitly when he invokes such concepts as change of register to deal with a voice-leading line that otherwise continues to nowhere.

42. See Schenker [1935] 1979, 10–21.

43. By "bop repertoire" I principally mean standards or jazz tunes that are used for bop improvisation, but the *Ursatz* forms to be discussed can also be found in the improvisations themselves.

44. Other analyses with blue background forms can be found in Martin 1988, 27.

45. For a discussion of structural levels in "Giant Steps," see Martin 1988, 23–5.

46. See Schenker [1935] 1979, 36–40.

47. This is Schenker's strategy in [1935] 1979, 144–5, where he applies his conceptual model to the themes under consideration rather than entire pieces. Schenker points out that sets of variations are often founded upon "a gradual increase in the motion, that is, progressing from larger to ever smaller note values." (144) This strategy occurs in jazz through the idea of "building" a solo.

48. Owens expresses a similar opinion in "Charlie Parker" 1974, 1, 227.

49. The idea of a thematic pattern applies to larger compositions as well, though they are not at issue here.
50. "All the Things You Are," (Kern, Hammerstein), 1939.
51. "Over the Rainbow," (Arlen, Harburg), 1939.
52. For more on the Palestrina curve, see Jeppesen 1970 [1946], 48–52. Strategies of open and closed space are developed in greater detail in the "Implication-realization" model of Eugene Narmour (1977) and Leonard Meyer (1973). This model has been applied to bop melodic lines by J. Kent Williams (1988) with useful results, especially in the area of showing how similar "gap-fill" patterns underlie these melodic lines. The Meyer-Narmour model works quite well here because of its focus on the spatial and rhythmic implications of melody.
53. Hierarchical approaches to the analysis of rhythm are developed in Cooper-Meyer (1960) and Lerdahl-Jackendoff (1983), and provide a basis for the Meyer-Narmour model discussed in the previous note.
54. Kernfeld 1983, 1988, and Gushee 1981.
55. Kernfeld 1983, 12.
56. Hodeir 1956, 144.
57. Kernfeld 1983, 8–9, makes a similar point with Sonny Rollins's "Blue 7" and "Vierd Blues."
58. But this should be approached with caution as well: all artists work in their own way, depending on their talent, goals, experience, style, temperament, and other such personal factors. Hence, even if through some mysterious process one could know exactly what Parker was thinking, it seems unlikely that thinking similar thoughts would produce improvisation equally brilliant. A well-known corollary: the best musicians have not always made the best pedagogues.
59. The preceding discussion of intention, relatedness, and value, summarizes a well-known position in aesthetics, and is included because, to my knowledge, these issues have not been raised with respect to jazz improvisation, formula and motive, and their particular difficulties. Critics insisting on objective analysis of the artwork in question have called those not agreeing guilty of the "intentional fallacy." This point of view was much associated in the 1930s, 1940s and 1950s with the "New Critics" of literary theory such as T. S. Eliot, John Crowe Ransom, and Cleanth Brooks. Gennari (1991, 459), in discussing jazz criticism in general, points out how detailed musical analysis of solos as self-contained aesthetic objects is similar to the work of the New Critics and is associated in jazz preeminently with the work of Gunther Schuller. For an influential formulation of the intentional fallacy from the point of view of philosophical aesthetics, see Wimsatt-Beardsley 1946. Although these authors focus on poetry, their argument gains still greater force when applied to instrumental music, an art form normally devoid of cognitive or referential meaning.
60. While retaining Owens's "M." for clarity in referring to his list of "motives" (1974, 2, 1–10), I shall consistently use the word "formula."

61. Gushee 1981, 240–1. Page numbers are from the Porter reprint (1991).
62. Gushee 1981, 244.
63. Kernfeld 1983, 26–7.
64. A "turnaround" or "turnback" is a prolonging series of chord substitutions in lieu of a single harmony. For example, an eight-beat tonic B♭ chord might be altered to B♭-Cm7-F7-C♭7 (two beats per chord) to create harmonic interest and a feeling of motion before the arrival of another B♭ tonic. Turn-arounds normally function as introducing or "setting up" the next section of the form.
65. Tiny Grimes Quintet: "Red Cross" (Charlie Parker), recorded for Savoy, September 15, 1944 (WOR Studios, New York City). Two takes: S5713-1 and S5713-2. Charlie Parker, alto saxophone; Clyde Hart, piano; Tiny Grimes, guitar; Jimmy Butts, bass; Harold "Doc" West, drums. Available on Savoy ZDS-5500.
66. For commentary on the early commercial recordings with the Jay McShann band, see Koch 1988, 22–40. Private recordings of Parker that precede the Tiny Grimes sessions also exist; for a listing, see Saks 1989, 1–4.
67. Owens's formula M. 40A. Many of the phrases of "Red Cross" can be derived from Owens's list and are cited in order to show that the original thematic material is evoked *despite* the use of formula—that thematic reference occurs through the choice and combination of these smaller-scale formulas. For detailed general study of the formulas in B♭ rhythm changes, see Owens 1974, 1, 98–107.
68. It is also Owens's formula M. 35. Its use here is thematic.
69. Not appearing in Owens's formula list (1974 2, 1–10), it was perhaps played too infrequently. He does point out, however, that the " . . . phrase recurs occasionally in later recordings in this category [i. e., B♭ rhythm changes]." (1974 1, 99)
70. The phrase leading to D5 in m. A3-3, then F5 in m. A3-4 may have been a final attempt to achieve the effect of a large-scale form before the solo closed.
71. The A2 section of the "Shaw 'Nuff" solo, as will be seen in the next example, also begins by establishing the higher register, then proceeding down to the register of the solo's opening. The downward direction of much of Parker's melodic exposition is a regular feature of his style.
72. The phrase in mm. B-5,6 of take 1, ending awkwardly, is a possible miscalculation.
73. Dizzy Gillespie's All Star Quintet: "Shaw 'Nuff" (Parker, Gillespie), recorded May 11, 1945, for Guild (New York City). Charlie Parker, alto sax; Dizzy Gillespie, trumpet; Al Haig, piano; Curly Russell, bass; Sidney Catlett, drums. Available on The Smithsonian Collection of Recordings, CD 2502.
74. To clarify this point further: the solos examined in this section have the same basic harmonic layout (rhythm changes), but slight harmonic differences

based on what is actually played by the rhythm section. None of these harmonic differences seem to have influenced the structural direction of Parker's solos; instead, structural differences are based on the motivic qualities of the original melodies.

75. In his formula list, Owens gives the F4 and D4 as F♮4 and D♮4, contrary to how I hear the solo, but the notes, admittedly, are indistinctly played. In "Thriving on a Riff," (Ex. 3–7), Parker plays M. 9 in the first take at m. 2A2-3. Here, the pitches are more clearly heard as F♮4 and D♮4.

76. See Owens 1974, 1, 105–7, where he shows typical B♭ rhythm-changes formulas in context. Bars A1-5,7 of "Shaw 'Nuff" can be seen (p. 106) as an approximate composite of formulas M. 10 and M. 6A.

77. The first four bars of the bridge are duplicated in the "Red Cross" takes, as discussed earlier.

78. Charlie Parker's Reboppers: "Thriving on a Riff" (Parker, Gillespie), recorded November 26, 1945, for Savoy (WOR Studios, New York City). First and Third takes: 5852-1, 5852-3. Charlie Parker, alto saxophone; Miles Davis, trumpet; Sadik Hakim, piano; Curly Russell, bass; Max Roach, drums. Available on Savoy ZDS-5500.

79. Only the first and third takes are relevant; take 2 was a false start. The same tune was later recorded as "Anthropology," the more familiar title.

80. Other small-scale thirds that unify the original melody: D4-C4-B♭3 (m. A1-1 to m. A1-4), m. A2-7: E♭4-D4-C4, m. A2-8: A3-B♭3-C4, m. B-1: F♯4-G4-A4, m. B-5: E4-F4-G4, from m. B-3 to m. B-4: B3-A3-G4, from m. B-6 to m. B-8: B♭-D-C. The end of the bridge is linked thematically to section A3: m. B-7: D4-C4-B3, m. B-8: C4-B♭3-A3, then in m. A3-1: D4-C4-B♭3. The end of the bridge, m. B-8: C4-B♭3-A3, is the retrograde of m. A2-8, which introduces the bridge. Other details worth noting: the G3 to F♯3 to G3 between m. A1-5 and A1-8 echoes an octave lower the F♯4-G4 of m. A1-7 to m. A1-8; the bridge adds a new voice-leading line at A4, which eventually proceeds through the G4 of m. B-5 back to the F4 of section A3.

81. Parker's solo playing and writing style are generally quite similar. In this case, the connections between melody and improvisation are even more specific, as will become clear in the analysis.

82. This phrase, listed by Owens as M. 44, is taken from the clarinet solo of the traditional Dixieland standard, "High Society." So yet again the inclusion of a well-known formula evokes the original melody.

83. Owens's M. 9, heard earlier in "Shaw 'Nuff."

84. The second run is Owens's M. 41.

85. Harrison (1976, 17) points out other internal correspondences in the solo: for example, the descending chromatic lines heard in mm. 1A1-3,4 m. 1A2, 4, and m. 1A3-4,5. His discussion of Parker formulas generally corroborates material from Ch. 2; in particular, he notes that some formulas are so simple as to allow "almost infinite variation" and calls them "basic shapes" (17).

86. Charlie Parker Sextet: "Crazeology" (Benny Harris), recorded December 17, 1947 (WOR Studios, New York City), four takes. Charlie Parker, alto sax; Miles Davis, trumpet; J. J. Johnson, trombone; Duke Jordan, piano; Tommy Potter, bass; Max Roach, drums; Available on Stash ST-CD—567/68/69/70.

87. Apparently the "crazy" aspect of the tune, although the original title of the tune was "Little Benny."

88. Quintet of the Year: "Wee" (Gillespie) recorded live at Massey Hall, Toronto, May 15, 1953. Charlie Parker, alto saxophone; Dizzy Gillespie, trumpet; Bud Powell, piano; Charlie Mingus, bass; Max Roach, drums; Available on Original Jazz Classics CD-OJC-044.

89. Live performances often feature exceptionally exciting playing. Studio recording often squelches spontaneity, given its hushed, almost antiseptic atmosphere, lack of audience response, and the necessity of coolly analyzing the playback of each take—often by production staff *and* players. Yet it can be argued that the best jazz recording from the point of view of the long-lived structural qualities of the solos themselves takes place in the studio. On some live performances, the spontaneity and excitement insufficiently compensate the lack of forethought and balance more characteristic of studio work. (This topic will be alluded to again in Ch. 6.) "Wee" is an exception: it is both exciting and spontaneous, while structurally up to the level of Parker's studio performances; for purposes of space, I only hint at some of these qualities in my discussion.

90. Charlie Parker Quintet: "Lester Leaps In" (Young), recorded live at the Rockland Palace, New York City, September 26, 1952. Charlie Parker, alto saxophone; Walter Bishop, piano; Mundell Lowe, guitar; Teddy Kotick, bass; Max Roach, drums. Available on Hipsville/Rhino CD R2 70198.

91. Charlie Parker Quintet: "Embraceable You" (Gershwin, Gershwin), recorded October 28, 1947, for Dial (WOR Studios, New York City). Two Takes: D1106-A and D1106-B. Charlie Parker, alto saxophone; Miles Davis, trumpet; Duke Jordan, piano; Tommy Potter, bass; Max Roach, drums. Available on Stash CD ST-CD-567-68-69-70, and on The Smithsonian Collection of Recordings, CD 2502. (Stash CD lists Oct. 26, 1947, as the recording date.) Transcription of take 1 based on previous transcriptions by Jimmy Giuffre and Zita Carno in Koch 1975a, 80–5, and Tirro 1977, 375–6. Transcription of take 2 by the author, based on an earlier, unpublished transcription by Josh Atkins.

92. There are other studio recordings based on the changes of "Embraceable You": "Meandering" and "Quasimodo."

93. Parker relies on motivic formulas to a considerably lesser extent here than in rhythm changes. "The slow tempo permits Parker longer than usual amounts of time to think of new phrases; consequently fewer applications of his stock motives occur." (Owens 1974, 1: 149). Owens then proceeds to point out a few of the recurring ideas.

94. Since the sections in ABAC form are somewhat less clearly demarcated than in AABA form, the measures for this analysis, and some others, will be numbered from 1 to 32.
95. Even the sound of the recording is very different, as if microphones had been adjusted. Perhaps Parker changed his reed as well.
96. Charlie Parker with Strings: "Just Friends" (Klenner, Lewis), recorded for Verve, November 30, 1949 (Mercury Studios, New York City). Charlie Parker, alto sax; Stan Freeman, piano; Ray Brown, bass; Buddy Rich, drums; Mitch Miller, oboe; Meyer Rosen, harp; Jimmy Carroll, arranger-conductor. Available on Verve CD 837 141-2.
97. As in "Embraceable You," prominent motivic formulas occur less frequently than in the rhythm-changes pieces. For this reason, the analyses to follow concentrate on relationships to the original melodies. "
98. Without the strings, presumably, there was no reason for the band to follow the original chart.
99. Koch points out (1988, 211) that Parker, in his recording at Birdland on March 24, 1951, seems to *base* his solo on the classic studio solo—that is, Parker "concocted variations upon former variations, forming a 'building' effect." This has long been the case in jazz performances—a legacy as old as King Oliver's "Dippermouth Blues" of 1923: once a definitive version of a solo has been recorded, audiences expect to hear it live, and may be disappointed it the soloist tries a fresh approach.
100. Charlie Parker Quintet: "Just Friends," ("Pop Goes the Weasel" quotation), recorded (probably) early June, 1950, at the Café Society (Downtown), New York City. Charlie Parker, alto sax; Kenny Dorham, trumpet; Al Haig, piano; Roy Haynes, drums; Tommy Potter, bass. Available on Mark Records MG 101.
101. References to the melody now assume it to be transposed to A♭ major.
102. Parker's quotations will be discussed in the concluding chapter.
103. Charlie Parker's Reboppers: "Koko," (Charlie Parker), recorded November 26, 1945, for Savoy (WOR Studios, New York City). Two takes, 5853-1 and 5853-2 (the first a false start). Charlie Parker, alto sax; Dizzy Gillespie, trumpet; Sadik Hakim, piano; Curly Russell, bass; Max Roach, drums. Available on Savoy ZDS-5500 and on The Smithsonian Collection of Recordings, CD 2502 (master take 5853-2 only).
104. A famous story, often repeated, surrounds Parker and "Cherokee," which probably originates in the Levin-Wilson interview of 1949 ([1949] 1994, 24). According to the authors, Parker found a major inspiration in the development of bop style in "Cherokee": "Working over 'Cherokee' with [guitarist Biddy] Fleet, Charlie suddenly found that by using higher intervals of a chord as a melody line and backing them with appropriately related changes, he could play this thing he had been 'hearing'. Fleet picked it up behind him and bop was born." But "Cherokee" *already* uses chordal extensions! It is probably the case that Parker found a way to expand his im-

provisational style by making use of what was already present in the song's melodic structure. Further, the authors do not quote Parker; instead they paraphrase his comments, making any assessment of his meaning even more difficult. For a further paraphrase of this quotation with an expanded historical context, see Hentoff-Shapiro 1955, 354.

105. Unknown Ensemble: "Cherokee" (Ray Noble). Porter (1993, 224) lists Minton's as the probable recording site. Available on Stash 542.

106. There are other large-scale connections to the original as well. "Cherokee" features a large-scale $\hat{3}$-$\hat{2}$-$\hat{1}$ form with the prolonged $\hat{3}$ sharped to $\sharp\hat{3}$ at the beginning of the bridge. Parker's solo conforms to this basic shape; moreover, the $\hat{3}$-$\hat{2}$-$\hat{1}$ close of the *Ursatz* occurs in both the D5-C5-B♭4 and D4-C4-B♭3 registers in his final A section.

107. Charlie Parker Quartet: "Star Eyes" (Raye, DePaul), recorded March–April, 1950, New York City. Charlie Parker, alto saxophone; Hank Jones, piano; Ray Brown, bass; Buddy Rich, drums. Available on Verve CD 837 141–2.

108. Parker Quintet: "Star Eyes" (Raye, DePaul), recorded February 18, 1950, at the St. Nicholas Arena, New York City. Charlie Parker, alto saxophone; Red Rodney, trumpet; Al Haig, piano; Tommy Potter, bass; Roy Haynes, drums. Available on JWS Jazz Workshop CD 500.

109. The 12-bar blues form appears in Ex. 2–2. For further discussion of the paradigm, see Martin 1988, 25–6.

110. Correspondingly, the popular-song repertoire is closer to the European basis of jazz through its use of functional harmony and melodies whose voice leading depends on these harmonies.

111. See, for example, "Just Friends," (Ex. 4–5), in which the progression of the background in Parker's solo was found to depend on *implied* melodic voice leading in the original melody.

112. "Usually" qualifies this statement because blues heads can be written with extensive harmonic functionality based on the circle of fifths. For example, "Blues for Alice," to be seen below (Ex. 5–5).

113. "Cool Blues" (Charlie Parker), recorded for Dial, February 19, 1947 (MacGregor Studios, Los Angeles). Charlie Parker, alto sax; Erroll Garner, piano; Red Callender, bass; Doc West, drums. Available on Stash CD ST-CD-567-68-69-70.

114. A strategy for listening to Parker's blues work might include discovering how Parker works with the figure defined as Owens's M. 10a, since it is so pervasive.

115. According to Koch (1988, 92) and the notes to the recording.

116. Charlie Parker All-Stars: "Perhaps" (Charlie Parker), recorded for Savoy, September 24, 1948 (Harry Smith Studios, New York City). Charlie Parker, alto sax; Miles Davis, trumpet; John Lewis, piano; Curly Russell, bass; Max Roach, drums. Available on Savoy ZDS-5500.

117. It would be interesting to study these and other multiple takes to see if any general conclusions could be drawn from Parker's dealing with an annoy-

ing and persistent technical problem. The takes for "Perhaps" are referred to by the numbering on the complete Savoy Studio sessions.

118. Charlie Parker and His Orchestra: "Au Privave" (Charlie Parker), recorded for Verve, January 17, 1951 (New York City). Charlie Parker, alto sax; Miles Davis, trumpet; Walter Bishop, piano; Teddy Kotick, bass; Max Roach, drums. Available on Verve CD 837 141–2.

119. Charlie Parker Quintet: "Blues for Alice" (Charlie Parker), recorded August 8, 1951 (New York City). Charlie Parker, alto sax; Red Rodney, trumpet; John Lewis, piano; Ray Brown, bass; Kenny Clarke, drums. Available on Verve CD 837 141–2. Transcription (unpublished) by Lothar Sieb.

120. Charlie Parker Quintet: "Bongo Bop" (Charlie Parker), recorded for Dial, October 28, 1947 (WOR Studios, New York City). Two takes, D1102-A and D1102-B. Charlie Parker, alto sax; Miles Davis, trumpet; Duke Jordan, piano; Tommy Potter, bass; Max Roach, drums. Available on Stash CD ST-CD-567-68-69-70. (The liner notes list Oct. 26, 1947, as the recording date.)

121. "Now's the Time" (Charlie Parker), recorded for Verve, July 30, 1953 (Fulton Recording, New York City). Charlie Parker, alto sax; Al Haig, piano; Percy Heath, bass; Max Roach, drums. Available on Verve CD 837 141–2.

122. The first excerpt given of Parker's solo in Ex. 5–7 (second staff) is related to Owens's M. 2B. Hence, a formula with intimate connection to the theme is chosen as the very beginning of the solo. Compare this to the beginning of Parker's solo on "Au Privave," Ex. 5–4, where the same motive is chosen: yet in "Au Privave" the phrase is ended on A4-F4-G4-E♭4: eighth notes taken directly from the third bar of the original melody. Hence, again, the formulas chosen are ones that can be adapted to the thematic context at hand.

123. Charlie Parker All-Stars: "Cheryl" (Charlie Parker), recorded May 8, 1947 (Harry Smith Studios, New York City). Charlie Parker, alto sax; Miles Davis, trumpet; Bud Powell, piano; Tommy Potter, bass; Max Roach, drums. Available on Savoy ZDS-5500. Transcription (unpublished) by Adam Hoffman.

124. Koch points out (1988, 92) that the "Cool Blues" riff is itself derived (quoted) from Parker's solo on take 4 of "Yardbird Suite," recorded March 28, 1946. Parker's quotations will be discussed further in the concluding chapter.

125. Charlie Parker All-Stars: "Parker's Mood" (Charlie Parker), recorded for Savoy, September 18, 1948 (Harry Smith Studios, New York City). Five takes. Charlie Parker, alto sax; John Lewis, piano; Curly Russell, bass; Max Roach, drums. All takes available on Savoy ZDS-5500. Take 5 available on The Smithsonian Collection of Recordings, CD 2502. For a transcription of take 5 (the issued master), see Tirro 1977, 379–80.

126. Takes 1 and 3 are false starts. Take 4 is cut off after Lewis's piano solo. Of

the two complete takes, 2 and 5, only the latter contains the introductory figure as coda.

127. Not contained in take 2, but possibly intended, since Lewis concludes with a tentative G-minor chord, as if he expected Parker to come in.

128. Even the famous first chorus of "Parker's Mood" contains references to the D-C idea, though they are less convincing than on the final chorus. For example, the opening melodic figure (mm. 1-1 to 1-3) emphasizes D4 as the on-the-beat pitch and the pitch the riff closes on. In mm. 1-4 to 1-5, the emphasis turns to the triplet 32nd C5-D♭5-C5, a modification of the C-D idea. When the tonic returns in m. 1-7, the focus returns to D4. So much of the chorus is unified through a large-scale motion from D to D♭ to D, with embellishment of the D♭ by C.

129. When they are present, of course. As seen earlier in "Embraceable You"(Ch. 4), slower improvisation may feature fewer motivic formulas.

130. Parker's resolution of his lines' voice-leading implications has been pointed out by other writers, e.g., Koch: "This characteristic of building lines so that they result in perfect musical resolutions is evident through all of Parker's improvisations." (1975a, 63)

131. As pointed out in Ch. 1, these remarks confirm observations by Owens as well as other writers.

132. Depending on the tempo, the principal subdivision of the beat may imply a triplet feel: the faster the tempo, the more the line approaches even subdivisions (usually eighth notes).

133. Other, more "immediate" qualities of Parker's style that account for his appeal include control of tone color, excitement in virtuosity, sensuousness of expression, and the timing and general layout of the phrases.

134. See Martin 1988 for the paradigm of circle-of-fifths voice leading in jazz that shows this pattern of resolution.

135. See Koch 1988, 283.

136. In an interview with Marshall Stearns, Charlie Parker relates being laughed off the bandstand since he could only play "Honeysuckle Rose" and the first eight bars of "Lazy River" (1950, Philology W 57-2). Whether true or dramatized for the sake of the interview, the story shows that in his *earliest* musical education, Parker was learning standards that featured simple harmonic motion and, especially in "Lazy River," strong circle-of-fifths harmonic patterns. This training obviously influenced his later preference for such progressions as the basis of his improvisational style. Parker's device of substituting "different changes" over the existing chords of an improvisation is also conservatively harmonic: the voice leading of the superimposed changes is patterned very simply so as not to interrupt the flow of the underlying progression. Compare "Red Cross," take 1, mm. A2-1 to A2-4, in Ch 3.

137. The motive of "Cool Blues," as was noted earlier, was itself derived by quotation of an earlier Parker improvisation. As Patrick points out, "Of

special interest is the appearance of short melodic ideas in the solos which later became incorporated in Bird's composed themes." (1990, 20.)

138. Such as the "Pop Goes the Weasel" quotation heard in "Just Friends—Café Society 'Pop'," Ex. 4–6. Incidentally, it would be instructive to evaluate the wide range of musical styles referenced by Parker's quotations: their sources include popular songs, opera, "light classical" melodies, children's ditties, and even Stravinsky, as pointed out by Patrick (1990, 20).

139. Identifying intentional quotations is not unlike searching for melodic sources of improvisational ideas that seem original. Giddins points out that the opening phrase of "Embraceable You," take 1, may have been taken from the tune "A Table in the Corner" (Sam Coslow), which was recorded by Artie Shaw (1981, 115–6). And Bill Kirchner notes that the opening idea of the "Embraceable You," take 2, is quite similar to "Bill" (Jerome Kern) from *Showboat* [private conversation]. Whether these sources are convincing or not, the validity of the thematic analysis is unaffected; for even if Parker's ideas are consciously or unconsciously based on these prior melodies, Parker's choice of them in the first place—like his choice of formula—seems based on creating cogent thematic relationship to the head.

140. See Chap. 5.

141. See Chap. 4.

142. Further investigation of this hypothesis would be a welcome extension of this study.

143. Then further, as noted in Ch. 4, the interrupted first take of "Koko" shows that the players definitely had "Cherokee" in mind and had just played it.

144. Koch (1974, 1975a) analyzes Parker's chord-scale preferences in detail and so demonstrates what particular kinds of melodic usages Parker applies to various harmonic and formal situations. The discussion of formula to follow focuses on the larger-scale issues developed in and raised by this study.

145. Hence, the lineages of soloists on various instruments can be traced (as, say, from Armstrong to Eldridge to Gillespie) with relatively little actual lick duplication, though clear indebtedness in a more general sense.

146. A term used by Sudnow (1978).

147. I recall arguments with musicians trying to decide the exact notes played in a passage—we might finger the passage mentally, then see if it felt "natural."

148. Another analogy that comes to mind is speed chess: the very best players are not always the best at the slower game.

149. Though not always, of course. Take 1 of "Embraceable You" (Ex. 4–2) is generally considered superior to take 2 (Ex. 4–3).

150. The most obvious instance of this is the inappropriate quotation.

151. It would not be surprising that some jazz improvisers find directly developing the motives of the head tiresome. Despite the excellence of much of the jazz and popular repertoire, it tends to be over-familiar. Further, the melodies themselves are often constructed internally through repetition, variation, and sequence, that is, they are already "developed."

152. Before the 1950s, of course. Since the 1950s, the increased artistic awareness among jazz musicians and the expansion of recording time have led soloists to experiment more with thematic development. In extended playing, they seem better able to develop the material consciously, yet integrate it with their own melodic sense as revealed by their melodic patterns, or formulas. Further, Kernfeld points out that the historical shift to modal jazz, then to free jazz releases the player from focusing on "the impossibly difficult task of spontaneously linking motivic development to fast-moving harmonies" [private communication]. The interest in motivic development has fine-art implications and can be related to the gradual evolution from popular to fine-art culture in many of jazz's substyles.

153. In addition to Kernfeld (1983) and Gushee (1981), which were discussed in Ch. 2, other studies include Smith (1983).

154. Lord 1960, 142.

155. Lord 1960, 47.

156. Taplin 1986, 68.

157. For example, see Shive 1987.

158. Taplin 1986, 68.

159. See Finnegan 1977 and Stolz-Shannon 1976.

160. For a useful summary of the controversies in oral poetry, see Lloyd-Jones 1992. Another controversy is the extent to which Homer was an individual artist rather than a compiler-editor of a tradition.

161. Lloyd-Jones (1992) notes that "Alfred Heubeck in his introduction to what is now the standard commentary on the *Odyssey* stated his belief that the great epics must have been composed with the aid of writing, but was willing to concede that this could not be proved. If he had lived to read Shive's book [(1987)], I believe he would have stated this conclusion firmly." (55)

162. See Shive (1987), Griffin (1986), and Heubeck-West-Hainsworth (1988).

163. Perhaps, though, even Ellington's "written jazz" can be seen as part of the oral tradition since it was conceived for specific players rather than universally for some generic instrumental ensemble.

164. Though implicit in the discussion, it should be emphasized that it is the nature of the formulas and the structures in which they are embedded that establishes the genre of the work as popular or fine-art. Blues formulas, for example, exemplify popular art, whereas licks derived from Indian music and heard in Philip Glass's operas or John McLaughlin's improvisations suggest the fine-art tradition, probably because of their exotic quality in a Western setting.

165. The continuing if not increasing popularity of Wagner's work, too, perhaps derives from its feeling of ritual, an element not otherwise prominent in late nineteenth century music.

166. The fine-art to popular gamut is also a function of social intent: a work recorded by an orchestra will be received and perceived differently from one appearing on a rap label — irrespective of the expressive content of the work.

Index

accents, 6–7, 54ff, 57. *See also*
Parker, Charlie, accents
"All the Things You Are" (Kern,
Hammerstein), 32, 33
analysis, methods of, 13–20, 20–26,
28–34, 138n33
Anstieg, 47
"Anthropology" (Parker, Gillespie).
See "Thriving on a Riff"
"Au Privave" (Parker), 105–6,
146n122
"Autumn Leaves" (Mercer, Prevert,
Kosma), 9–10, 12, 29–31, 32, 33

Bach, J. S. (*Partita II in D Minor for
Violin*), 15–17
background. *See Ursatz*
Basie, Count, 129
Benedetti, Dean, xi, 1
"Bill" (Kern), 148n139
the blues, 3, 9, 11, 99–100, 136n12
"Blues for Alice" (Parker), 105–6
"Bongo Bop" (Parker), 106

Cage, John, 113
"Cherokee" (Noble), 93–95, 115,
144n104
"Cheryl" (Parker), 107–8, 114
Coltrane, John, 126, 128–29. *See also*
"Giant Steps"
comping, defined, 137n20
"Cool Blues" (Parker), 33, 100–102,
107–8, 114, 147n137
counterpoint. *See* voice leading
"Crazeology" (Harris), 6, 64–66

development, thematic, 4, 35, 111,
120, 135n4, 148n151, 149n152

diminution, 30, 32, 77, 84ff, 95–97,
112, 119, 137n28

Eastwood, Clint, xi
Ellington, Duke, 123, 149n163
"Embraceable You" (Gershwin,
Gershwin), 28, 29, 33, 71–82,
119; original melody, 71–72; take
1 solo, 72–78, 148n139, 148n149;
take 2 solo, 78–82, 148n139,
148n149
Evans, Gil, 123
extended-chord tones. *See* tensions

form, 9–13, 136n14; AABA, 41–42;
ABAC, 29, 71; blues, 9, 11; theme
and variations, 30–32, 139n47.
See also rhythm changes
formulas, melodic, 1–3, 4–5, 34–39,
54–57, 59, 66, 70, 99–100, 101,
111, 115–19, 121–22, 125–30,
141n67–69, 142n75–76,
142n82–85, 143n93, 145n114,
146n122, 149n164
fundamental line (*Urlinie*), 28–32,
139n36. *See also Ursatz*

Gennari, John, 140n59
Gershwin, George, 71, 135n11. *See
also* rhythm changes
"Giant Steps" (Coltrane), 10–13, 29
Giddins, Gary, xi, 148n139
Gillespie, Dizzy, 137n19
Glass, Philip, 126, 149n164
Grimes, Tiny, 42
Gushee, Lawrence, 37

harmonic vs. linear function, 26–28

harmony, 5–6, 9–13, 14–15, 21–23, 41, 142n74. *See also* Parker, Charlie, harmony
Harrison, Max, 2, 142n85
head, defined, 135n3
Heckman, Don, xi
"High Society" clarinet motive, 60, 142n82
Hodeir, André, xi, 135n10
"Honeysuckle Rose" (Waller, Razaf), 147n136
"How High the Moon" (Hamilton, Lewis), 136n12

"I Can't Get Started" (Duke), 137n19
improvisation: thematic, 1–5, 38, 135n4; types of, 34–39. *See also* development; Parker, Charlie, thematic reference
intention of the artist, 3, 35–37, 140n58–59. *See also* development; Parker, Charlie, thematic reference

jazz in Western culture, 122–28, 149n152
"Jazz Me Blues" (Delaney), 10
"Just Friends" (Klenner, Lewis), 29, 32, 82–93, 145n11; Café-Society ("Pop") solo, 89–93; original melody, 83–84; studio solo, 84–89

Kernfeld, Barry, 34, 37–38, 135n4, 149n152
Kirchner, Bill, 148n139
Koch, Lawrence O., xi–xii, 103, 144n99, 146n124, 147n130, 148n144
"Koko" (Parker), 93–95, 115

"Lazy River" (Carmichael, Arodin), 147n136
Lerdahl, Fred, and Ray Jackendoff, 138n33
"Lester Leaps In" (Young), 68–69, 70, 101
Lloyd-Jones, Hugh, 149n160–61
Lord, Albert, 121

Mahler, Gustav, 127
McLaughlin, John, 149n164
McShann, Jay, 93, 129
Meyer, Leonard, 140n52
Monk, Thelonious, 137n27
motives, 33–34, 35, 38–39; general development of, 4, 35

Narmour, Eugene, 140n52
notation, 7
"Now's the Time" (Parker), 107–8

Oliver, King, 144n99
oral-epic poetry, 121–22
oral vs. written tradition, 113, 117, 122–25. *See also* oral-epic poetry
"Over the Rainbow" (Arlen, Harburg), 33
Owens, Thomas, xi–xii, 2, 4–5, 37, 54–57, 59, 66, 99–100, 101, 136n16, 141n67–69, 142n75–76, 142n82–84, 143n93, 146n122

Palestrina curve, 33, 140n52
paraphrase, 34, 35, 38, 82, 96–97, 112, 119, 130
Parker, Chan, xi
Parker, Charlie: accents, 20, 54, 56, 57, 111–12; compositions, 113, 142n81; development, avoidance of, 4, 111, 120, 148n151, 149n152; formulas, use of, 1–3, 111, 115–18, 120–21, 128–30; harmony, 113, 147n136; phrasing, 54ff, 112; quotation, 92–93, 107–8, 114, 146n124, 147n137, 148n138–39; research on, xi–xii; sense of swing, 19–20, 112; style of, 3, 17–20, 111–15, 118–21, 128–30, 141n71, 142n81; thematic reference, 48, 70, 82, 97–98, 109, 114–15, 118–21, 148n139; voice leading, 4, 17–20, 22, 111–12, 147n130, 147n136. *See also* formulas, melodic
"Parker's Mood" (Parker), 107–9, 114–15, 146n126–147n128
Parry, Milman, 121

Partita II in D Minor for Violin (Bach), 15–17
Patrick, James, xi–xii, 2, 135n11, 136n12, 147n137, 148n138
Paudras, Francis, xi
"Perhaps" (Parker), 102–5
primary tone (*Kopfton*), 23, 51, 139n36
prolongation, general discussions of, 9–13, 15–20, 24–25, 27, 28–32; through neighbor tones, 14, 17–20, 24–25, 32, 57; through passing tones, 14, 15–17, 32

quotation, 92–93, 107–8, 114, 146n124, 147n137, 148n138–39

"Red Cross" (Parker), 23–24, 35, 69, 120, 147n136; original melody, 42–43; take 1 solo, 44–47; take 2 solo, 47–48
rhythm, 33, 54ff, 101, 138n33, 147n132. *See also* accents
rhythm changes, 3, 9–10, 41–42, 115, 135n11
Rink, John, 137n28
Rollins, Sonny, 135n4

Schenker, Heinrich, 4, 13–14, 71, 136n16, 137n17, 137n28, 138n29, 138n33, 139n36–37, 139n41, 139n47
Schoenberg, Arnold, 127
Schuller, Gunther, 135n4, 140n59
Shaw, Artie, 148n139
"Shaw 'Nuff" (Parker, Gillespie), 17–20, 21–22, 24–26, 32, 35; improvisation, 51–57; original melody, 48–51
"Skippy" (Monk), 137n27
"Star Eyes" (Raye, DePaul), 95–97
Stearns, Marshall, 147n136

Stravinsky, Igor, 126–27
Strunk, Steven, 14, 137n22, 138n31
Sudnow, David, 116
"Sweet Georgia Brown" (Bernie, Pinkard, Casey), 10

"A Table in the Corner" (Coslow), 148n139
Taplin, Oliver, 121
tensions or extended-chord tones, 14–15, 21–22, 25, 113
thematic pattern, 4, 23–25, 27–28, 32–34
thematic reference. *See* Parker, Charlie, thematic reference. *See also* improvisation, thematic; development, thematic
"Thriving on a Riff" (Parker, Gillespie), 57–64; original melody, 58–59, 142n80; take 1 solo, 59–61; take 3 solo, 61–64
Tirro, Frank, 135n11
transcriptions, 5–7, 137n18
turnaround or turnback, 41, 141n64

Urlinie. See fundamental line
Ursatz, 23, 26–32, 127, 139n36

variation form, 30–32, 139n47
voice leading, 4, 13–22, 138n33. *See also* Parker, Charlie, voice leading

Wagner, Richard, 127, 149n165
"Wee" (or "Allen's Alley") (Gillespie), 66–69, 143n89
"What Is This Thing Called Love?" (Porter), 136n12
Williams, J. Kent, 140n52

Young, Lester, 37. *See also* "Lester Leaps In"

About the Author

HENRY MARTIN is a faculty member of the Mannes Conservatory's Jazz and Contemporary Music Program at the New School for Social Research, where he directs the curriculum in music theory and composition. He has also taught jazz history and theory at Princeton University. His teachers have included Milton Babbitt and David Del Tredici. With a Ph.D. from Princeton University and degrees from the University of Michigan and Oberlin Conservatory, he has pursued a dual career as a composer-pianist and as a music theorist specializing in jazz and the Western tonal tradition. His compositions have been performed extensively throughout the United States and are published by Margun Music. His compact disc, *Preludes and Fugues,* has recently been released by GM Recordings. Mr. Martin has published numerous articles on jazz and music theory in such journals as *The Annual Review of Jazz Studies, Perspectives of New Music,* and *In Theory Only.* He is an Associate Editor of *The Annual Review of Jazz Studies.* His first book, *Enjoying Jazz,* was published in 1986. He spoke on Charlie Parker at the American Musicological Society's national convention in Pittsburgh in November, 1992.

Made in the USA
Lexington, KY
12 June 2013